Adventures of a No Name Actor

Adventures of
a No Name Actor

Marco Perella

BLOOMSBURY

Published by Bloomsbury, New York and London.
Distributed to the trade by St. Martin's Press.

Library of Congress Cataloging-in-Publication Data

Perella, Marco.
Adventures of a no name actor/by Marco Perella.
p. cm.
ISBN 1–58234–155–9 (alk. paper)
1.   Perella, Marco. 2. Actors–United States–Biography. L Title.

PN2287.P386 A3 2001
791.43'028'092–dc21
[B]   00–140116

First U.S. Edition
10 9 8 7 6 5 4 3 2 1

Typeset by Hewer Text Ltd, Edinburgh, Scotland
Printed in the United States of America by
R.R. Donnelley & Sons Company, Harrisonburg, Virginia

Contents

Foreword
Molly Ivins

Who wants to read another book by some rich, famous, successful actor? Especially when we can hear from Marco Perella instead. He's un-rich, un-famous and perfectly hilarious. Besides, he wrote this book himself.

Marco Perella is to-die-for funny. For reasons I have never understood, as his true tales become more bizarre and woeful, they just get more hilarious. Marco is not the actor who was the understudy when the star broke his leg and couldn't go on: Marco is always the guy whose leg gets broken. I think it's typecasting: directors just look at him and think, 'Future mincemeat.' He almost became the only human being ever killed by a fake tornado. Marco's life is full of improbable disasters that begin with something like, 'So then I get the drop on Billy Sabbath in a cheesy motel and torture him until his fellow alien killers come to the rescue, at which point I'm supposed to jump off the second-story balcony and run away with super-human speed.'

Marco is also locally famous for his splendid psychotic villains. You have to hear him explain these plots to believe them: 'After the third successful kidnapping of Renee, I leave her in the capable hands of Big Dexter with an ice hook. Dexter winds up frozen on an icy carpet of comic books.' It's not that Marco Perella is recounting this as the biggest pile of bull doody he's ever had to deal with: he's always seriously working at making his psychotic killer more human, more sympathetic, more fully developed. Part of the hilarity of these stories is that Marco never stops working at his craft: 'Tonight James Coburn gets impaled on his backyard satellite dish. My part consists of continuing to be dead.'

For years, Marco has written round-robin letters to a large circle of friends describing his professional misadventures, to our recurring delight. When 'resting' between jobs, Marco occasionally writes up the latest lunacy in which his chosen Art has involved him and passes it along via the U.S. mail. I think it was his account of having been hired to be a Greek god on Olympus for the Dell Computer company's Christmas party (the guests thought he was a biblical prophet) that first moved me to urge him to make a book of the letters. So now he's what Texans call An Arthur.

Marco's cheerful stoicism in the face of a lifetime's largely unrewarded dedication to the theatrical muses is partly what makes him so funny. That and the fact that he's Texan. A person could be an unknown actor in New York City and still take himself seriously. In Texas, you've got to have a sense of humor. As he once philosophically remarked of a failed effort to get a cowboy part: 'It's my name. Everybody thinks all Italians are from New York. It doesn't matter that I'm third-generation Texan and used to work on a ranch and rope dogies. One great-grandfather from Palermo and they'll never let you on a horse.'

I have often listened to the lovely James Lipton of the

Actor's Studio interviewing wildly successful actors for the Bravo television network, and I always think, 'Marco's stories are much better than this.' Marco has played the Easter Bunny, a Jungian archetype, done daytime soaps, corporate gigs and commercials for unlikely products. He's been in memorably bad made-for-TV movies and was in the funniest production of *Streetcar Named Desire* in the history of small theater.

OK, so he's actually been in real films with important people like Kevin Costner and Clint Eastwood. This makes no difference: the best stories are still the epic disasters. The French cinematographer who screams, '*Non! Non!* Geeve me 40K! *Merde!* Eets raining. We're fooked. Fooked!'

I read somewhere that the secret to great comedy is continuing to be perfectly serious in the midst of absurd conditions. It's a description of Marco Perella's life. Not since the Little Tramp has a sweet, sincere fellow been regularly pitchforked into such hysterical imbroglios. It should be required reading for all aspiring actors. What a treat of a book!

A Drowning Fool

IT WAS THE JESTER SUIT that they really hired. I know that. But it'll be me in the suit and I'll be great and I'm getting paid and now my résumé will have that nice fat entry under 'Feature Films'. So what if I'll be wearing clown makeup and floating down a river and nobody could possibly recognize me. I'm in pictures now, dammit.

The movie is called *Fandango*, and it's the story of four high school chums who drive off into west Texas looking for one last adventure before they all go to Vietnam. It stars a bunch of unknowns. Some kid named Kevin Costner has the lead. Judd Nelson is one of the chums.

The director went to the University of Texas film school and did a short that won some kind of award. The powers that be liked his *Fandango* script and just like that he's in the Big Time.

At the audition they're looking for people who can do costumed characters for a dream sequence. I show up in my outfit: a red and yellow jester suit with blue tights, plus blue medieval cap and bells.

It happens I've had an act for the last couple of years at the Texas Renaissance Festival. I appear as Womba the Fool. What I do is get people out of the audience to portray various kings and queens of England. I turn them upside down and carry them around the stage while I spout British poetry. The highlight comes when I do Henry the Eighth and get his six wives lined up and go down the line beheading them and taking outrageous liberties with their breasts:

> Anne Boleyn was his second wife,
> He swore to cherish her all his life.
> But seeing a third he wished instead,
> He chopped off poor Anne Boleyn's head!

Everybody is so drunk at the Renaissance Festival that I somehow get away with it. I was drawing big crowds until a local newspaper printed a photo of me pursuing a ripe Texas woman across the stage. Some dope had captioned it. '*Womb* the Fool cavorts.' After that I started getting *really* big crowds.

The season prior to *Fandango* I shared a stage with some low-rent juggler/magicians from California named Penn and Teller. We'd alternate shows all weekend. Penn's act is to juggle apples and spit apple core all over the front rows. Teller does this real spooky thing where he swallows a bunch of needles and then gulps down some thread. Then of course he pulls a whole line of threaded needles out of his mouth.

Pretty good act. They said they were looking to do Broadway, but I don't know.

My *Fandango* scene is to be shot on the absolute first day of filming, and I report to the set, down on the Guadalupe River south of Austin. What we're after is a dream sequence wherein Judd Nelson processes his meaningless teenage existence just before he goes off to war and starts living his meaningless adult existence. There's this little wooden bridge over the river, and Judd is supposed to hunker down there while all these Jungian archetypes from his subconscious come floating out of the mist, down the river and under his prone body.

That's what I am, an archetype. I've done some research on Jungian archetypes and the jester is in there somewhere, I'm sure of it. Anyway I'm a medieval Fool and that's in the Tarot, and I know the Tarot is archetypal as all hell so I'm sure I belong somehow.

Our band of floaters . . . make that Actors . . . consists of five archetypes. Besides me, there's a Big Businessman (wearing a three-piece suit), a Doctor (wearing one white smock), and a Blond (wearing two large breasts). Plus a seventy-two-year-old actress named Bea Townsend who wears an authentic nun's habit.

So, we archetypes are supposed to float in a straight line right down the center of the river. As we come to the bridge, Judd Nelson is going to reach down and try to save us, but before he can we're to be swept under and drowned in the restless currents of Judd's subconscious mind. (What can I say, our director has a Vision.)

The problem with actually shooting this scene is that it's spring and the Guadalupe is full of extremely cold, fast-moving water. I mean, it's a *river*, right?

So first of all we have to wear wetsuits under our costumes. That's a bit of a problem for Bea, because they don't really make wetsuits for portly nuns. Anyway, dressing takes a couple of hours. They also have to rig up a raft for the camera out in the middle of the river so they can get those really sexy low shots of bobbing jester heads coming out of the fog. That takes the rest of the morning, and then it's lunch.

All the archetypes waddle off to eat in our squeaky rubber underwear. People are excited about the first day of the shoot, and we're all introducing ourselves to everyone. Kevin Costner is walking around subtly reminding everyone that *he* is the star and not Judd Nelson, even though we just happen to be shooting Judd's big scene on the first day.

In my naïveté I have brought my wife, Diane, along with me to witness my first movie triumph. That's her over there now, being hit on by Judd Nelson. At least he has good taste.

By two o'clock we're finally ready to get in the water. All five of us are well bloated from the huge, meaty, catered lunch we just ate. The Blonde thinks it might help us float. On the other hand, if our distended bellies rupture the wetsuits it might help us founder.

(Does it penetrate into my cap-and-belled head for a moment that my entrance into the world of motion pictures is to be in the guise of a Drowning Fool? Is it an augury? An omen? A portent?)

Our costumes are adjusted and we slip into the river upstream from Judd and it's freezing and the current is too strong and we are immediately swept downstream, under the bridge, and on to the Gulf of Mexico. The grips have to intercept and haul us ashore before we take leave of Texas.

The brass are outraged.

'You were supposed to wait for "Action" and then float in a straight line!'

We timidly point out that the current is pretty strong and it's just a little difficult to maintain nautical bearing.

Our director is not amused. His Vision is at stake. Besides, he has evidently tried to quick-grow a mustache to give himself some heft, and his upper lip hasn't cooperated. I can tell he's trying to compensate by reaming lesser creatures . . . meaning us, the local talent. He thinks this will prove to the Hollywood producers that he's a strong director who can control the set with an iron hand of which John Ford himself would have been proud.

We take another two-hour break while they rig a cable out in the middle of the river for us to hold on to until they yell 'Action'. Back in we go. We space out on the cable every ten feet or so and are instructed to maintain that exact spacing until we reach the bridge. Then, when Judd has finished reaching down to us, then and only then are we allowed to drown. There will be absolutely no drowning before that point.

Fire up the fog machines! Oh boy, everybody's getting excited now. The assistant director is yelling through his megaphone for more fog. The Visionary is up on the bridge behind Judd, spurring him on to new levels of emotional commitment. Another hundred people or so have shown up, lining the river bank to root us, the subconscious flotilla, on to glory.

'ACTION!'

'CUT!' The director is gesticulating.

'Hands! Hands! I need to see your hands! What's the matter with you people?'

It seems that we all have our hands down under the water holding on to the cable so we can guide ourselves downstream while still maintaining our sacred spacing. So, instead of bobbing archetypal heads, we're all hunched down in the water like beavers with just our front teeth showing. Nothing at all like floating Jungian archetypes.

We have to practice. I, ever the innovator, develop a system of straddling the cable with my legs and kind of scrotuming myself down the river with the current. This way my hands are free to hold up beside my clown-painted face in bemused helplessness. Big points from the brass.

'Yeah! That's it! That's it! Everybody see what the jester's doing? Like that! Like that!'

The rest of the flotilla try to master my technique. The Blond and the Business Man and the Doc do OK, but Bea keeps getting her nun's habit fouled on the cable. She twists around and is pulled under with an ominous sucking sound. Also, although her name may suggest beatitude, Bea can't seem to achieve the blank-faced, dreamlike quality considered so desirable in an archetype. She persists in clenching her teeth in terror as she fights to keep her head above water. They finally give up and let her float off to the side where the current is weaker.

The director is upset that his Vision is being compromised. Now it's so late that they call it a day.

Bright and early the next morning we are back in the drink. I have been moved to the place of honor: first man on the cable.

'FOG ON!'

I bob and drift until I am right under Judd Nelson. He extends his hand to me, imploring me to save myself, but I stare blankly up at him as I sink beneath the turgid waters.

Pretty good, but now they are enamored of this look on

my face where my mouth is opened in a startled O like in the *Scream* painting by that Scandinavian guy. It looks great until just before I go under, but then I tend to close my mouth in a craven attempt at self-preservation. This spoils the effect of a soulless wraith from Judd's subconscious; I merely look like some crazy swimmer trying not to drown.

It won't do. It just won't do.

Never fear. I am a budding artist already dedicated to his craft. Give me another chance.

We all drag ourselves back upstream against the current until we are in our places once again. Fog . . . bob . . . drift . . . hands waving piteously . . . eyes blank and wide open . . . every mouth an O. Judd reaches down and . . . Glug! I become one with the river, at least two gallons of which are now definitely part of me.

I sputter off to the side while the rest of my fellow bathers reach the bridge behind me and attempt to duplicate my technique.

'CUT!'

Cheers all around. Now all we have to do is the same thing again for what seems like forty times until the camera has covered the scene from every conceivable angle.

The hour grows late and daylight fades. Golden Time. When director's fancies grow tumescent with technicolor.

'Once more! Right away! Right away! Hurry people, we're burning daylight!'

My blue tights have long since shredded from gripping the steel cable between my thighs. My hands look like frozen chicken parts. I am bilious from imbibing the less than limpid waters of the Guadalupe.

I glance over at Bea. Her lips are blue. She looks real bad. The set doc has noticed this too and I see him come over to the director and tell him, 'I think we should get her out.'

The Visionary merely stares at him and yells, 'ACTION!'

And the cast sails on. At Golden Time plus thirty minutes they finally call it quits, and we drag ourselves ashore. All the Hollywood people are pounding one another on the back. We costumed wraiths are instantly forgotten. The Businessman's three-piece suit has shrunk. The Blond's big red lips are locked in a rictus smile of frozen horror.

The wetsuit people start ripping our clothes off. They want their equipment back as soon as possible so they can start drinking.

Friday night they throw a cast party at the hotel. It's a big hoo-haw with a live band. Diane and I show up and do our country swing out on the floor. I see a producer admiring our style. He calls us over and asks us if we can teach Kevin Costner and his love interest how to dance like that. The climax of the picture has them doing the fandango and nobody is really sure what that is. But they want it to look good.

Sure thing, got your fandango right here. Where do we sign up? Actually I haven't a clue what a fandango is either. But I have good ears and can hear opportunity knocking.

The producer is a little distracted because he's about to marry Meg Tilly. But he does set us up with one of his minions, who introduces us to Costner. We make a date to start dance classes when the Stars are not on the set.

I ask several revelers how the river sequence came out.
Nobody is very forthcoming on that subject.

The next evening we show up at a room in the hotel
and Kevin Costner meets us there. We congratulate Kevin
on his good fortune in bagging this role and he confides in
us that not only does he have the lead in *this* picture, he has
a glorious part in something called *The Big Chill*. This
work of art will come out soon and the studios are calling
and he is, in general, slicing through the butter of life with
a very hot knife. Since we are obviously expected to be
impressed, Diane and I make soft, reassuring cooing
sounds and touch him reverently on his godlike shoulders.

Suzy Amis, the costar, now joins us. We turn on the
tape and start teaching the basics of country western
dancing. I show the moves with Diane and then dance
with Suzy and walk it through with Kevin. Kevin dances
with Diane a little bit and then tries it with Suzy.

After an hour Diane and I exchange covert glances. It is
obvious that Kevin will need many, many lessons. Diane
whispers to me that he's possibly the worst dancer she's
ever danced with.

'Not that it matters,' she adds.

Naïvely I ask what she means.

'Oh . . . nothing.'

Diane drifts back over to Kevin and continues drilling
the steps. She looks a little flushed.

Suzie on the other hand, is a good dancer and is learning
quickly.

It is decided that since the company is moving to a new
location in South Texas, I must be officially hired as
permanent dance teacher and brought along. I have to
go get a deal memo signed, promising I will be paid a

certain amount. They will call me (don't call them) when they're ready for more lessons.

When they finally do call it is two weeks later. They want me to get on a plane that leaves in one hour. At this point I make an unforgivable mistake. I say, 'Wow, I have a job to do this afternoon. Can I fly out tomorrow instead?'

Never say no to Hollywood. I get the axe immediately. Evidently there are dance teachers in South Texas too, and they don't have to be flown in and put up in hotels. So there goes the choreography credit. But I console myself that at least my Drowning Jester scene will surely loom large in the history of Texas buddy movies.

Word eventually trickles down that something happened to the footage on the river-dream sequence. Rumor has it that in all the excitement somebody didn't check the gate of the camera and water bubbles ruined the film. They had either to reshoot or cut the scene. Having spent a bundle on two days at the Guadalupe, the Budget Suits say cut.

No dream sequence. Two days of Near-Death Experiences in the river for Nada.

Judd Nelson's subconscious mind is rendered mute, my first feature film credit has been negated, and Carl Jung sleeps with the fishes.

Glumly, Diane and I go to see *Fandango* when it comes out. But it is a very enjoyable movie. The dance sequence at the end is terrific. Spectacular, even. And Kevin Costner dances like Baryshnikov.

Rites and Wrongs of Passage

IF YOU SAW the character name 'Wendall Hitch', on the cast breakdown of a movie you would immediately think . . . Evil Minion! And of course you'd be right. Evil Minions are my meat.

I am an actor who, with hair slicked back, can handle such roles while waiting to star in a remake of *High Noon*. At any rate, regionally speaking, romantic leads starve while Evil Minions thrive. And there will always be a warm spot in my heart for Wendall Hitch, because Wendall was my breakthrough role.

Breakthrough to what, you might ask. Well, to more Evil Minion roles. I've now played dozens of them. And although I play a good guy now and then, the good-guy parts are seldom as juicy.

All of which speaks volumes about my career trajectory. The rocket goes up – veers sideways when the boosters disengage – and tries to maintain enough velocity to prevent orbit decay.

Let me give you a brief idea how I became a Regional Actor and occasional Co-Star without leaving Texas and never having to take a job in a cubicle. Then we'll get back to the story of Wendall Hitch and the Hollywood Heavies.

One thing about film acting that's really different from

other jobs is the glimmer factor. What I mean is that up there on screen, glimmering year by year, floats a glamorized, self-inflated portrait of yourself as a Big Star.

When I started out, I saw myself as another, slightly more ethnic Harrison Ford. A little time went by, a little of the glimmer wore off, and then I began to see myself as maybe another Robert Duvall. Not a glamour puss but a hell of an actor. A few more years in the business and I'll probably start glimmering what an admirable career Slim Pickens had. Not that there's much call for Italian cowboys.

I know what you're saying: 'Why didn't you go live in New York or Los Angeles where the big roles are? You could have gotten into one of those Mafia TV shows!' Good question.

It might be convenient (though misleading) to say that I put off taking all the courses I needed for a theatrical major at Stanford until my senior year. Then I wouldn't have to admit that I didn't take a single acting class at Stanford because it was the sixties and I went to a few too many Grateful Dead concerts and decided to leave school after my junior year and go live in a log cabin.

I spent ten years in Taos, New Mexico, where I did construction work and fought forest fires to earn a living. I was also, on occasion, a lead singer in several rock bands that played the Southwest circuit.

One of these bands was a heavy metal group called Cosmic Showers. We rehearsed in an old movie theatre owned by Dennis Hopper. The guitarist was a Chicano named Kardo Romero who played so loud that plaster chips would actually fall off the adobe walls. Our drummer, Ernie, once called me a wimp because I couldn't scream loud enough to be heard over the amps. We had a fistfight and I punched him out, proving I was man enough to scream. Our group chemistry improved after that.

My interest in acting was not aroused until a friend talked me into auditioning for a part in a local production of *West Side Story*. I got the part of Riff. Dennis Hopper brought Neil Young, Dean Stockwell and Russ Tamblyn to see the show. Tamblyn played Riff in the movie version, and after the show he came backstage and embraced me with tears in his eyes. (I prefer to think they were tears of rapture.) This went to my head, and I was fatally stricken with acting lust.

I played Jesus in *Godspell*, with Cosmic Showers serving as the orchestra. (Think 'Day by Day' at forty decibels.)

I slicked my hair and grew a pencil mustache for *Guys and Dolls* and scared my girlfriend so bad she left me.

In a parody play written for the D.H. Lawrence Festival in Santa Fe and Taos (featuring Ian McKellan and Liz Taylor), I portrayed an Edwardian old maid who inserts a live wire into her teapot and jolts herself into orgasm. (My girlfriend came back because of that one.)

Of course the financial resources for actors in northern New Mexico were limited. I was still fighting forest fires. One time I made it back late from a fire and did *Robin Hood's Sherwood Scandals* in tunic and soot-face.

Determined to follow my acting bliss, I decided to move to Austin. After ten years in the mountains I suspected I might experience culture shock in a big city, but I had friends in Texas (the state where I was born), and Austin had three or four paying theatre companies at the time. I figured it was a good place to start.

Just before I left Taos I met my future wife, Diane. The timing was lousy. I was determined to relocate. She made the mistake of visiting me in my new Texas home and I kidnapped her. Soon her two kids were with us as well, and nuptials ensued.

I did a lot of theatre in Austin until I realized that, hey, you really *can't* make a living as a stage actor! I got an agent and started doing film and TV. I did commercials, industrial training films, student thesis films and the occasional bit part in actual Hollywood films. Hollywood films in Texas? Sure.

A lot of movies are shot on location in places like Texas, Florida, Arizona and North Carolina. *Terms of Endearment, JFK, A Perfect World, Lone Star* and *Places in the Heart* were made in Texas. Plus there are TV series like *Walker: Texas Ranger,* TV movies and lower profile independent films being shot here all the time. Although the leads for these projects are almost always brought in from L.A. or New York, it is often financially attractive to hire local talent to fill out minor roles such as villains, cops, lawyers, snitches and gun fodder.

It was the mid-eighties when I got the proverbial 'Big Break'. A bunch of us wrote and acted in a monologue play called *In the West.* For some reason this simple little raggedy-ass play with no sets became a huge regional hit and got written up in *Variety.* Before long we were invited to the Kennedy Center, where we performed before elite but adoring multitudes. I did two monologues in the play – a guard dog salesman and a high school football coach. Both of them were kind of funny/bad characters. Suddenly I was being called in to read for funny/bad characters in the movies. Soon I was doing featured parts and then . . . (trumpets please) . . . Costarring Roles!

At this point I could have conceivably gone to one coast or another with some cache. Why didn't I? Because I never really wanted to. (That's part of the answer; the other part is rental apartments, new schools, and day jobs.) People tend to assume that fame and stardom is the ultimate goal of any actor, but all I ever wanted to do was make my living doing what I loved and I was already doing that in Texas. The lifestyle suited us in Austin, where my wife also had an acting career going. I had a band on the side. It just wasn't that attractive to pursue the gold ring in brassy cities far away.

I'd been performing *In the West* in Dallas and some of the local casting directors had come to see it. One of them was casting a movie called *The Passage,* and when she saw me with my hair slicked back she called me in.

Normally I'm a fairly pleasant-looking person in a curly-headed, Mediterranean sort of way. But when I slick my hair back I can manage to look like a psychotic mole rat. This comes in handy for roles like Wendall Hitch, and I got the part.

Set in 1920s Alabama, *The Passage* is about Young Samson, who gets teased a lot because he's a long-haired, woodsy kind of fellow who lives in a cabin with his beloved grandfather, played by Brian Keith. They both work for the tough lumber boss played by Ned Beatty. Ned has a beautiful daughter played by Alexandra Paul, a future *Baywatch* babe. (The smart one.) Ned also has a toadie named Wendall Hitch.

The Passage is what you call an *independent* film. That means none of the Hollywood studios is paying for it. Rather, Young Samson is paying for it. Young Samson is from an oil family in Fort Worth. He not only wrote the script, but also made an easy casting decision as to who would play the lead.

He has also rented practically the whole East Texas town of San Augustine as the movie's location. This is a real old burg just north of the Big Thicket, with period buildings and an operating steam train that will figure prominently in the story.

I drive up from Austin and report to the location. My home for the next three weeks will be an old resort hotel out in the boonies. This place has been closed for a while and the production has rented it to house the actors. Each of us gets practically a whole wing to ourselves.

It is with some anticipation that I arrive at the dinner hour. I feel like a twittering teen. I'm about to meet real Movie Stars! Oh gosh! I sure hope they accept me! What if they want to talk Concept!

I stagger through the door of the hotel with three weeks' worth of luggage. I'm in some kind of anteroom, but it's so dark I can't see much. I start dropping my stuff in a noisy heap.

'Hello! Anybody home?'

Nobody seems to be extant.

Then I look off to the right and see one dim light shining in what seems to be a vast, dark room. The light hangs over a long Gothic dining table around which I presume are the faces of my fellow cast members. They gaze curiously in my direction. Lest they think I do not belong, I quickly identify myself:

'Hi! I'm Wendall!'

They don't exactly all jump up at once and pummel me on the back and say, 'Welcome, Comrade!' In fact there's no response at all. Ned Beatty, especially, has that 'no vacancy' look about him. I try again:

'Wendall! In the movie!'

Finally Brian Keith addresses me:

'Close the door, Wendall, and come get some dinner.'

I obediently come to table. As I sit down, I start to introduce myself and explain that my actual *name* is not Wendall. But the familiar-looking woman next to me gives me the *shush* sign. She looks meaningfully down toward the other end of the table. Now I recognize her: Barney Miller's wife on TV! Barbara Barrie! I go into the classic goofball fan opening:

'Didn't you used to be on . . . ?'

Barbara shushes me again. Oh. I am beginning to think I must have interrupted something important.

Brian and Ned are locked in passionate conversation about . . . well, I guess they're talking about fishing. Yeah, that's it all right. Ned is telling a clever story about a big one he hooked in Tennessee. I turn back to Barbara and then look across the table at Alexandra Paul. She gives me a smile and rolls her eyes. We are evidently expected to remain silent.

The rest of dinner passes without any conversational input from anyone except Ned Beatty and Brian Keith. Ned tells flamboyant stories but seems to be addressing only Brian, as if they were alone. Actually it's more like he's giving a *performance* for Brian, who spends most of his time heartily consuming victuals but occasionally comments on one of Ned's remarks. The rest of us listen. I'm not sure yet what the deal is and at one point give a little chuckle and say something like, 'That certainly is funny, Ned!'

Beatty stares at me like I just passed gas in church.

Barbara is playing Ned's wife. After dinner she takes me aside and explains to me that Ned has some problems and gets very upset if anyone other than he or Brian speaks at dinner. That's because they're the big stars and Barbara, Alexandra and I are not quite on the radar of fame yet. 'I know it's ridiculous, but I'd rather just eat and not make a fuss about it,' she says.

Gee, thanks for the warning. I guess I'll go to my quarters and scourge my unclean flesh.

My first scene is at the train station. Alexandra is coming home from her school in the East and I, Wendall Hitch, am there to assist in baggage handling. I will assign a young buck from the local sawmill to load up the damsel's collection of fripperies. The young buck in question turns out to be Samson, who immediately falls in love with this fabulous creature who is so high above him. I will notice this and make him pay for his insolence. That's how movie plots work.

I go to wardrobe and get outfitted in period suspenders. Then to makeup to perform my magic hair-slicking metamorphosis. When I report to set Barbara is waiting for me: 'Ugh! Are you the same guy from last night? Wow! Stand back a little bit, will you? Listen, the director is a fool. Don't listen to a thing he says. You'll have to direct yourself. Just inhabit the character and do your best.'

What? Don't listen to the director? Oh jeez, what gives? This is my first big role. I am hideously conflicted. Maybe Barbara is insane.

Here comes Brian Keith. He says, 'Listen, Wendall, don't worry about the asshole director. The idiot doesn't have a clue. He wanted me to come out a week early so we could talk "Concept"! Ha! Can you imagine? Just do your best, son. You'll be fine. Jesus, what happened to your hair?'

It seems that Young Samson has hired his overaged acting teacher to direct this feature, but the guy has somehow failed to make a good impression on the cast. As a matter of fact, he is pretty much banished from the set after the first day, never to appear again while Ned or Brian are around. Over the next three weeks I will occasionally see him sitting by himself under a beach umbrella, far from cast and crew, pretending still to be the director. He'll even stand up and shout 'Action!' once in a while, just to keep his hand in. But nobody pays the slightest attention to the poor guy.

Meanwhile, I'm trying to inhabit my character. Ned Beatty quickly fills the director vacuum in this train station scene. This will be the pattern for the duration. Ned directs all the scenes he's in and Brian directs all the scenes *he's* in, and if they're *both* in the scene, well then, there'll be some discussion.

The train blows its whistle and steams into the station. Beautiful Alexandra steps down. I scuttle around for her bags. (Ned's direction to me has been clear and concise: 'Stop being taller than me, dammit!')

Scuttling helps to maintain my shrinkage. Actually this

works out well. Since my character is an obsequious toad licker, constant groveling fits right in. Likewise, it helps Ned get in character to order me around and belittle me in front of the crew. We have soon established an effective, symbiotic acting unit.

The shoot unfolds fitfully. The crew is schizoid from adjusting and readjusting to the different styles of substitute directors Ned and Brian. When neither of *them* are on the set, the very competent director of photography takes charge.

Young Samson also tries to direct, especially the love scenes with Alexandra. ('Take forty-four!')

Samson is catching on fast. Early on, we shoot a scene where his character gets so ticked off at Wendall that he almost crushes me like a grape. This is an essential scene for Wendall's motivation because it will lead to all kinds of dastardly revenge. However, Samson looks bad beating up a mole rat.

He decides to cut the fight and replace it with some more love scenes.

Off set, dinners are still surreal, but I'm starting to make friends with the cast. Alexandra Paul is refreshingly level-headed. She's charming and intelligent, and dedicated to her acting. She spends most of her free time swimming laps in the pool. She's maintaining that sleek look so essential for Hollywood Leading Ladies. (I'm over on the Sophia Loren side of things myself. I dread swimming and am naturally sleek, so I usually sit at poolside and drink.) Little does Alexandra know that her affinity for water will eventually make her fortune.

I've also buddied up with Brian. Brian is in his seventies now, and his career has been so long that he's worked with everybody. He was actually a child actor in silent films and got sick of the whole business early on. He got out of the Marines after World War II and was going to be a New York cop. Somebody offered him a summer stock acting job that paid a few dollars more than the cop job, so he got into acting again.

Brian maintains high good humor most of the time. He entertains us with tales of John Ford westerns. He laughingly informs me that the only people who will ever see *The Passage* are members of the country club to which Samson's father belongs. (He's right. Samson will refuse to accept the ritual screwing that seems to accompany the efforts of most independent filmmakers trying to get distribution. In protest he will refuse to release *The Passage*. Even on video.)

The only thing that gets Brian's goat is any mention of Brian Dennehy. He's convinced that he should be getting all the roles that are now going to Brian Dennehy.

Unfortunately, my relationship with my initial friend on the set, Barbara Barrie, has soured. This is because of tennis. Barbara is from the Hamptons or someplace like that, and her big deal is tennis. Since we have a lot of free time she recruits a foursome. There's me and Norman and Charlie. Norman plays the country doctor and Charlie plays the country preacher. They're staying at the hotel too, but neither one of them can stand Ned Beatty so they don't eat with us.

We play doubles almost daily. The problem is I'm not very good, and when I hit a bad shot I tend to cuss. When

I hit a good shot I also cuss. Cussing just seems to be my natural response to the game of tennis. Barbara doesn't care that I'm a bad tennis player, but she gets very huffy when I violate the sacred etiquette of the game. I don't know what the big deal is. Hasn't she ever seen McEnroe? Anyway, I enjoy cussing when I play tennis and I'm already taking so much crap from Ned that I'm not inclined to defer to Barbara. I cuss away. Poor Barbara is stuck with me if she wants a foursome.

Barbara also spends a lot of time lecturing the Texas crew on the rules of the Screen Actors Guild. The producers have talked a lot of film students into serving as cheap assistants on the set, and the kids don't really grasp the concepts of overtime, meal penalties and forced calls. (A minimum of eight hours of rest between two days of work and they have to feed us every six hours.) The students dread coming to fetch Barbara after she's been kept waiting for hours in makeup while the train gets up steam.

One morning she really let's everybody have it and tells one and all she won't report to the set until she gets a penalty check laid on her dressing table. Somebody has to go get Samson to write the check.

Ned is such a good actor that I begin to wonder if his imperious behavior is just character development. I mean, this nightly dinner performance can't *really* be an attempt to impress Brian, can it? Maybe his conflicted boss character is leaking into his psyche and he's lost in the Method.

I'm starting to have serious doubts about my commitment to Wendall. My natural tendency is to model myself after these master craftsmen. Should I be a toad-licker *all* the time to stay in character? But I have to wash my hair sometime, don't I?

Ned has formed a habit of donning an apron and serving food at the big on-set meal each day. He enjoys being a man of the people, I guess. He serves up the southern fried and jokes with the proletariat. This is peculiar because in private he's hardly the egalitarian. In fact, Ned is always referring to the locals who are working in the crowd scenes (extras) as though they were some nascent life form.

He tells the story about the time he hired a baby sitter and kept thinking she looked familiar. Then it came to him . . .

'That woman is an *Extra!* (Dramatic pause) . . . I went right home and got my kid!'

Although I don't realize it at the time, Ned's attitude is fairly typical in the business. Although extras are an absolutely essential component of making a film, almost everybody on the set treats them with contempt. The areas of the set where the extras stay are called 'holding pens.' Need I say more?

One night there's a local rodeo over at the fairgrounds, and I talk Brian into going with me. He's not sure it's such a good idea, but he'll try it.

Brian loves me now because I lent him my car to drive to Houston so he could visit an old drinking buddy. This saved him a hefty rental fee, and even though he is socking away half a mil on this three-week project, he *enjoys* saving money. (Depression kid. They never have enough.) He also loved driving my little ten-year-old Toyota. I guess a man who's been in Cadillacs all his life finds it novel to hunker down that close to the road.

We arrive at the rodeo and take our seats in the stands. There're about a hundred people there and just about all of them come over and get in line to ask Brian for autographs. Not just one signature each, either. 'Can you sign one for muh mother? And one for muh step-brother Alvin? And jus' one more for muh cousin Hilda over in Lufkin?'

Brian almost literally never sees the rodeo. And people couldn't care less. They are completely oblivious. Brian is a good sport, but I recall he did try to warn me. It's as though he's being consumed like free ice cream. And Brian Keith is not exactly at the top of his career: what must it have been like earlier? I arrive at a new appreciation for what people like Tom Cruise go through.

A big ol' country gal wants Brian to kiss her. No deal. 'I've been in these little towns before', he confides. 'There's always a jealous boyfriend with a monkey wrench.'

After a little more of this we decide to try a casual escape act and head for the car. We're ambling over by the bullpens when the amorous country gal makes her move. She leaps out of the dark, grabs Brian and starts kissing him. It doesn't matter to her that he's a seventy-year-old man. He's a *Star*, and by God she's gonna kiss him! Poor Brian just stands there and endures it until the gal has been thoroughly irradiated by the glorious aura of his celebrity. Finally she runs off giggling to her girlfriends.

Brian laughs about it as we drive home in my Toyota. 'You sure you want to be famous, son?'

In addition to avoiding all references to Brian Dennehy around Brian Keith, everybody has been very careful not to mention anything concerning pigs around Ned. This, of course, is in deference to his most famous role as the love interest in *Deliverance*. They're not even serving pork at meals. That's why it comes as a considerable surprise when Ned himself brings up the subject.

It's probably Wendall Hitch who instigates this incident. We're having some downtime on the set. (Waiting for the train to back up, no doubt. We've spent a cumulative week of shooting time waiting for the train to get in position.) In my continuing dedication to toad-licking I bring up the subject of *Network* and what a fine performance Ned gave in that movie. Ned proceeds to tell me how he 'really had his man in that part' and how it's one of his favorite roles. Then I get real dumb. I ask him what his *favorite* role is.

'Oh, I guess the pig thing in *Deliverance*.'

I keep on smiling. Ned continues, 'You know, the squealing wasn't scripted. That was *my* idea. The original script just had us rolling around in the woods. I thought it needed something so I suggested the squealing.'

'Wow! You thought it up yourself!'

'Yes. That's what made the scene memorable, I think.'

'Oh, you bet! Memorable for sure!'

'My career really took off after that movie. Funny how just one scene can make such a difference. Because of that scene I bought a farm in Kentucky.'

(Don't say it. Resist . . . resist . . .) 'A pig farm?'

The Passage is drawing to a close.

Alexandra's character gets knocked up by Young Samson when they get caught out in the woods by a rainstorm.

(Whenever it rains in a movie, there's sex.) Ned disowns her, thus denying himself access to the passel of adorable grandchildren she and Samson start producing. Alexandra is fulfilled even though she has to live in a hovel instead of in the big house with her dad and mom.

Brian's grandfather character has a heart attack while he's clearing land and does such a poignant death scene that everybody cries. I ambush Samson in town with a gang of lumberjacks, and we beat him up for no discernible reason since they cut the scene that was supposed to inspire my vengeance. It does give Samson the opportunity to fight bravely against impossible odds and then go home to Alexandra so she can lovingly daub his bleeding lip.

My spouse comes to visit for the last few days of the picture. I haven't really explained the peculiarities of our dining regimen here at the resort, and Diane starts talking to somebody at the table while Ned is telling one of his stories. Everybody tenses and Ned turns toward her with disapproval. Diane has no idea what the hell is going on. I manage to whisper to her:

> ME: Nobody's supposed to talk! Just Ned!
> DIANE: What are you saying? Why?
> ME: I'm not certain. We have to know our
>   place, I think.
> DIANE: That's the most insulting, outrageous
>   thing I've ever heard in my life! Nobody's
>   going to tell *me* not to talk!

And she proceeds to interrupt Ned at every opportunity. She holds forth on topics that she knows nothing about and in general has a wonderful time flapping her lips together until she totally dominates the conversation.

The power center of the whole dining group has shifted. Barbara, and Alexandra are starting to look at Diane as if she is Gloria Steinem. Brian is enjoying the hell out of the situation and Ned, strangely enough, turns into a good listener.

We're packing up to leave when I drop by Ned's room to say goodbye. He tells me, 'That wife of yours is one of the most beautiful, intelligent people I've ever met! What an impressive person! I have new respect for you, Marco.'

Oh the irony! All my toad-licking has earned me nothing. Only through my backbone-endowed spouse have I garnered any respect at all from this man. I vow never to buy into anybody's star trip again.

I say goodbye to Brian as well. He asks me what I'm doing next and I blurt out that I've been cast in a picture with Barbara Hershey and Brian Dennehy. Oops!

He gets a stricken look on his face. 'Brian Dennehy. Always Brian Dennehy.' I quickly add that it's only a TV movie and that seems to make him feel better.

Brian thanks me again for the use of my car and asks for my headshot so he can recommend me for a role 'when they need a *good* actor.' He's bullshitting me, but it's still nice. Then he leaves me with these words of wisdom:

'Remember the young bull and the old bull. The young bull says, "I'm gonna run down the hill and screw one of those cows!" The old bull says, "I'm gonna *walk* down the hill and screw 'em *all!*" '

Darn good advice, don't you think?

Maniac in the Mirror

TV MOVIES ALL SEEM to have the same name. That's because they're usually about sex and crime. So they always try to get words in the title that bring such thoughts to the fore. *Desire* is a perennial buzz-word. Likewise *Evidence, Killing* and *Seduction. Body* works for both sex *and* crime, so that's a big one. The TV movie geniuses have learned that if they mix and match these words in the titles, America will tune in.

Evidence of Love, Shadow of Desire, Desire in So-and-so, Killing in So-and-so, Seduction in So-and-so . . . they just keep recycling these names. I might have been in three TV movies that were at one point or another called *Body of Evidence* until Madonna made a feature film and got the final rights.

Everything is 'based on a true story' and then changed to include more sex and more murders. You've got Plot A and Plot B.

Plot A is: A lovely, slender woman in her late twenties sleeps with a handsome guy and he turns out to be a stalking psycho killer. She has to get violent and the authorities don't understand.

Plot B is: A lovely, slender woman in her late twenties sleeps with a handsome guy and *she* turns out to be a stalking psycho killer. She has to get violent and the authorities don't understand.

I've done Plot As with Kim Delaney and Nicolette Sheridan. I did a Plot B with Barbara Hershey, where she has an affair and then chops up the guy's wife with an ax. Barbara won an Emmy for that. They started out calling it *Killing in a Small Town* and then changed it to *Evidence of Love* and then changed it back. Why escapes me.

Another Plot B is *Body of Evidence*. (Number two or three, I'm not sure which. Madonna bent some knees and they changed the title to *Seduction in Travis County*.)

In a small Texas town, a lonely lady falls in love with a married lawyer. She seduces her handyman into killing the lawyer's wife for her so she can have the lawyer. The authorities don't understand.

I get the plum role of the handyman. Along with it comes the unlikely name of Clancy Pogue.

I wear what I think is a Pogue-ish T-shirt to the audition, along with one of those fake panther tattoos. I slouch and drawl as somebody might if he were named Pogue. George, the Hungarian director, eats it up.

The whole Texas accent thing makes these foreign directors lose their minds. First day on the set George takes me over to meet the star, Leslie Ann Warren. He presents me to her like a piece of Valentine candy.

'Look fot I got for you! Tok for her, Marco! Tok!'

'Howdy, ma'am. Pleezed tuh meet yuh.'

Leslie giggles with pleasure.

George is trying to cheer Leslie up. She's a little depressed right now, I think. Either that or she's mooding up for her role as a murder-hatching psycho she-bitch seductress from hell. They've had to hire six extra people from her entourage to make sure she has the right hair and the right exercise and eats the right food.

For moments of extreme stress she carries a Walkman so she can listen to a special tape. I wonder what it is? Maybe it's New Age music: *Sounds of the Waterfall . . . Listening to the Light . . . Distant Elves . . .* Maybe it's reggae that soothes her? Or a Tony Robbins motivational tape?

I think Leslie is just a naturally delicate person and needs a lot of soothing.

First we shoot the butt-twitching scene. I'm down on the floor in Leslie's kitchen, fixing an electrical socket or something, and she's listening to grinding rock music while she makes lemonade in the blender. Leslie's trying to recruit me to be her evil henchman. Her plan is to mesmerize me with sex. They've got her in these tight blue jean shorts with a blouse tied up around her pancreas. She dances around the kitchen twitching her butt in my face.

Leslie may be delicate, but the girl can sure twitch. Her figure is decidedly womanly. As Roy Orbison might say, 'Mercy!' Very little acting is required on my part. She gives me a glass of lemonade and goes all googly-eyed, and I am ready to kill.

Since they never shoot movies in chronological order, next up is the scene where the cops come busting into my dingy handyman's pad and beat me up and haul me away for murdering the lawyer's wife. The cops are being played by a bunch of my local actor buddies, and since they're jealous that I landed the best part out of all the

Texas actors and got to have Leslie Ann Warren twitch her butt in my face, they make sure the beating part is realistic. Again, very little acting is required on my part. I am dragged down the hall by my hair and so to jail.

For the jail scene I get to wear an orange jumpsuit like real prisoners. I'm supposed to smoke a cigarette and confess that I did it for love. This means a big close-up for me, with all the Texas cop actors standing around wishing they had this part. (But there can only be one Clancy Pogue.)

Unfortunately this is a scene that *does* require acting, and here I run into trouble. I have somehow decided that the circumstance calls for volcanic emotion, and on the first take I screw my face up and try to squeeze out real tears.

'CUT!'

George takes me aside and earns his pay.

You mean I don't look like a poor, lovelorn dupe lost in the depths of demented devotion?

George patiently and gently explains to me that I look like a bad laxative commercial.

We do it again. This time I restrain myself and am content with a lip quiver that speaks volumes. Huzzahs all around.

And now for the wife killing. This takes place at one of the fanciest houses in Austin. I'm sure the owners thought it would be neat to have a movie shot in their house. They probably had no idea what a crew of forty could do to a wood floor.

Peter Coyote is playing the sexy lawyer, and we strike up a conversation about the old days in San Francisco, where we both experimented with alternative lifestyles. Or exploded the plastic inevitable. Or whatever the hell it was we were doing back then. I still haven't figured it out.

Peter's soon-to-be-wasted wife is being played by Jean Smart. It happens that Jean just had a baby, and she has a nanny on the set to hold her bambina whenever she has to be on camera.

What's supposed to happen is that I, Clancy Pogue, the slave of love, come to the front door and ring the doorbell with a fake flower delivery. When Jean opens the door she catches on that all is not well. She tries to slam the door, but I power my way in. (They want me to grunt animal noises during this part. They say they're going to synthesize these noises later to make a spooky sound track.) Then I am to chase Jean upstairs, blasting away at her with my pistola.

So we shoot the front door scene and all goes well, except they aren't happy with my animal noises. They make me record a few extra grunts. These are called wild tracks, and everybody gets real quiet on the set while they stand around watching me growl and snarl.

It's time for the Art Shot. In every TV movie there is at least one Art Shot. That's because all TV movie directors want to be doing big-studio features instead, and they think that if they throw in an Art Shot somebody will see that they have serious talent.

George is not immune to Art Shot Syndrome, and being Hungarian the condition may be terminal.

In this case he has set the camera on the second floor looking down the main staircase in this fantastic home. There's a huge mirror on the first landing where the stairs make a ninety-degree turn and go on up to the second floor.

Jean is supposed to run up the stairs screaming bloody murder, with me in hot pursuit. Just as she crosses in front of the mirror I'm supposed to fire at her and *hit the mirror instead*. See, they've got the camera focused on the *mirror* seeing me in *reflection*, and when that bullet hits the mirror it goes all cracked and so does my image.

Voila! Art Shot!

Of course I'm not *really* going to fire a bullet at Jean Smart's head. I'm firing a *blank*, and at the same instant the explosives expert will set off a charge behind the mirror.

So the first time we try it, Jean runs up the stairs and I stop at the bottom. I shoot at the mirror. The explosives guy hits the switch. Nothing. It's a tough mirror.

So we try it again – same thing. And again.

By this time George is beginning to wonder about the explosives expert. There are deadlines to meet and the man can't even destroy a mirror. Besides, this is the Art Shot! Let's get with it!

Kid Dynamite doubles the charge. I fire the blank, he hits the switch, and . . . Double nothing. Evidently his expertise does not extend to antique Texas mirrors; the double charge makes not a dent.

Now George and all the brass are livid with rage at this poor guy. He hastens to guarantee that this time he'll crack my evil reflection for good. We hear him making noises behind the mirror. When he comes out this time he pauses by me, whispering, 'Why don't you move back a couple of feet on this take?'

What? I can't move back! I have to hit my mark so I'll

show up in the mirror and my image will be reflected correctly when the mirror shatters in a vivid metaphor for the fractured nature of evil! It's an Art Shot!

'OK', says Blast Master, 'but I just put seven charges behind that mirror, so at least close your eyes.'

OK. Here we go. Jean Smart and I take our pre-murder positions once again. Wait a minute. Seven charges? Close my eyes? That doesn't sound too good.

But Jean is running up the stairs, so I follow, aiming my gun at the mirror. Just before I fire I get that *This could be bad* feeling. Should I cut the scene? Or should I do my sacred actorly duty and forge through to the finish no matter what happens?

What would Robert Mitchum have done?

I pull the trigger.

Kapow!

Big slabs of glass containing my reflection slam me in the face. Actor down! Actor down! The uncrackable cracked. All over the stairs, all over the house, and especially all over me.

They check me over. The producers are pale with fear. But I'm lucky. Superficial wounds only. It must be that every one of those slabs of mirror hit me with their flat sides. I know it's incredible, but if I'd caught an edge it'd be *Night of the Living Dead* sequels for me.

Peter Coyote is appalled. 'How could they *do* that to you?'

Director George goes from apoplectic to apologetic. Captain Nitro is fired on the spot. And since I am evidently too healthy to file a glass action suit, the producers relax.

'New deal!'

We're moving upstairs for the climax of the scene. The crew bustles around making sure they grind the broken glass deeply into the fine wood floor.

Jean Smart is going to be hiding in the bedroom closet. I am going to bound across the bed in my work boots and capture her there. But it took so long to get the Art Shot that her baby is getting fussy. Jean has to stop and hold the little thing to settle her down. Before each take she hands the baby to her nanny and cowers down in the closet screaming, as I trampoline over to her hiding place and shoot her in the neck. I'm supposed to reprise my grunting animal noises and then emit a sort of evil yodel as I do these things.

A couple takes of this and the baby is understandably disturbed. She doesn't know it's just a movie. As far as she's concerned some maniac is attacking her mother. Jean is screaming, I'm screaming and the baby is screaming. Savage frenzy on the second floor!

I give it to Jean in the neck one more time and she does an interview with *Entertainment Tonight* and we finally go home.

Someday a repressed memory therapist will be hypnotizing Jean Smart's daughter and . . . Surprise! Clancy Pogue!

The big bar scene. Forty extras dancing. Fifty pipers piping, milkmaids milking . . . the works. They've got crew crawling all over the walls trying to light this cavernous old Sixth Street club in downtown Austin.

This is a scene where Leslie Ann tries to come on to Peter Coyote. Peter spurns her (even though he slept with her before) and goes righteously home to his wife. Leslie covets him, so she hatches her devious scheme of eliminating Jean Smart. And we know how *that's* going to come out. This is when Leslie comes over to me at the bar and asks me to come home and check her socket.

So everybody's preparing for this big scene when suddenly we hear: *CRASH!*

Here comes Leslie. She's mad as a wet cat.

It seems that the Little Black Dress she picked out for this scene was torn somehow, and now the wardrobe people are trying to get her to wear a replacement dress. But Leslie does not like the replacement dress. Trouble.

She stomps and yells and throws stuff until George clears the set. All the extras and crew have to go outside.

George tells me to stay because he thinks Leslie likes me after my heartfelt performance in the butt-twitching scene. He might need reinforcements. He goes over to salve the wounds.

I guess he says the right thing because Leslie finally calms down and puts on her Walkman earphones. She starts pacing around in circles trying to find a happy place.

Before he brings back the hundred and fifty people waiting out in the alley, George has Leslie and me rehearse the scene at the bar. He's trying to ease her back into harness.

I feel a certain measure of trepidation when he brings Leslie over to me. As a regional actor (translation: Hollywood nobody), my career hangs by a thread. Costars cannot afford to piss off a star. What if I look at her cross-eyed or something and she has another fit?

Not to worry. Leslie is soliciting my support.

'I think it's just awful when they say you can wear something and then they give you something else at the last minute. It's not fair, is it?'

'Absolutely not. I understand completely. I'm on your side. You can trust me— I'm not like the others.'

'Do you have someone in your life?'

'Beg pardon?'

'Are you married?'

'Uh, yes I am. For many years.'

'You're lucky. I don't have anybody and it gets real lonely.'

And she starts to cry.

This woman is a movie star and she makes tons of money. She's a good actress and she's beautiful. But it's not enough.

George and I pat her gently on the back and try to make her feel better. We assure her that the replacement dress looks real nice. I get her a tissue from behind the bar.

After a while the crew drifts quietly back on the set, the dancing extras go to their places and they turn on the music. Leslie and I do our scene. It goes well. And then she says goodbye and goes back to her trailer with her Walkman.

Another TV movie is in the can.

I go home and give my wife a great big hug.

Oliver the Lion King

SOME OF YOU may not understand how I get hired to be in all these fabulous movies. Do they call me up and say, 'Report to the set and be a movie star'? Nope. Do they just assign me a part because my résumé has ambience? Negatory.

What I have to do is audition for every part. Which is OK with me. I like driving in the personal ruts I've worn in the highways from Austin to Houston and Dallas. I *like* to audition. Way I figure, it's a chance to act, and that's what actors like best.

What happens is the local casting director sends a call out to various agents to assemble certain actors she knows or picks out from photographs. We all get appointment times to come read for a part.

The audition consists of reading a scene with the casting director while somebody tapes it. Then the casting director plays the tape for the director and various brass of the picture and they decide which ones they want to call back. A callback is really just a second audition much like the first except this time the director and producer, and maybe the writer and somebody from the network, are in the room watching you. Auditions are weird because sometimes you're reading a scene between a man and his horse and the casting director is playing the horse. But the main variable is always the director.

Sometimes you go into the room and the director hops out of his chair and shakes your hand. (Wow! Maybe he's interested in you!) He actually takes the time to look at your résumé and ask what you did in *Johnny Zombie*. He doesn't snicker when you tell him you carried a torch and marched around with a bunch of enraged townspeople shouting, 'Burn him! Burn the zombie!' Maybe this Sensitive Director will brief you on the character and ask if you have any questions about the script. Then he'll sit back, give you your moment and watch respectfully while you perform the scene. He'll shake hands again when you leave, and even if you don't get the part you've been treated with respect, like the artist you undoubtedly are.

That's what some directors do. Then there's Oliver Stone.

The Stoneleigh Hotel is one of the grand old hotels of Dallas. Having slipped below the radar of most business travelers on expense accounts, the Stoneleigh has been forced to cater to tourists who are looking for atmosphere. It also caters to movie companies, who rent several suites and call the whole hotel their production office.

That's the case with the movie *JFK*. Oliver Stone has brought his traveling circus to town and Dallas is aquiver. Big D is still supersensitive to the assassination, and everyone is quite concerned as to how the whole thing will be depicted. Oliver Stone has somehow gotten permission to use the actual Dealey Plaza and the infamous Texas Book Depository to restage the thing. Mucho buzz.

My fellow actors and I are camped out in the hall of the Stoneleigh, waiting our turn to see the Man. I'm auditioning for the part of an FBI agent who has an interview with a woman claiming to have seen Jack Ruby cruising the Plaza with a rifle a couple days before the assassination. I've got my gray suit on and my slicked-up, early sixties, government-issue haircut.

There's considerable nervousness in the hall. I mean, adrenaline is always in oversupply before an audition, but this is real damp-palms stuff. Word has gotten around that Oliver Stone is raging unchecked through the assembled auditioning multitudes. There has been rending and tearing. This works on the imagination until you can see him in there now, reaming somebody exactly like you. Or throwing away the script and telling you to improvise. Actors are coming out of the audition room and making bug eyes at the rest of us by way of warning.

I am not afraid. I have an Italian father. I've been yelled at by professionals. Besides, I've got it scoped. Oliver was in 'Nam, right? He's into this Marine thing. Auditions are like boot camp to him. Trial by fire and all that. He's trying to see what we're made of.

He's like a lion on the savanna, scaring hell out of the antelopes. If they run fast enough they get to eat grass again, but if one stumbles . . . Lion King moves in and disembowels it.

I can respect that.

Anyway, I am ready for Simba. I've lucked out and gotten a scene where my character gets real mad. So when my turn comes and I'm ushered into the Presence I'm already primed to come across as one fast antelope.

Oliver is sitting in a great big peacock chair that absolutely dominates the room. The man has actually made himself a throne. I resist the urge to fall on my face and grovel.

The motionless Stone says very little if anything to me. Dance, boy, dance. So I launch into my bit. Except when the script stops I'm just getting started. I'm supposed to be yelling at this witness, but since she's not there I'm kind of aiming my tirade in Oliver's direction. I go off on a complete improvisation, laced with the most colorful expletives I can pronounce. I'm stomping around and turning red and lacerating the air.

Finally I run out of gas and look up at the throne. As the Russians say, Is Miracle!

Oliver Stone, Lion of the Stoneleigh, is actually *beaming* at me! He's *laughing*! He *loves it*! I'm *hired*!

So after the running of the antelopes you probably think that Oliver backs off and gets all cuddly when we're actually shooting the movie. Well . . . not really. But I'm happy to report that he remains very amiable toward me during *JFK*.

I like to flatter myself that it's because he recognizes in me a fellow predator, but it's more likely that he craves the meat of elands and I'm more of a springbok.

My first day on the set consists of standing around watching them shoot the Dealey Plaza scene. Oliver has set up in a big tent about a quarter mile from the set. It's bristling with at least six different camera monitors. Oliver directs the scene from afar as the distant cameras pump visual information to him through massive cables snaking into his tent. This is the highest tech of the time, but he's so far away from the set that poor Oliver must be content to kick butt through his walkie-talkie.

My scene is shot in an abandoned office building in a cruddy little room. For this scene Oliver is right in here with us. Everything goes well except I have no idea what my character's motivation is. (That's your Method talk right there, Baby!) Ed Neal, who played the hitchhiker in *The Texas Chainsaw Massacre*, is my FBI cohort. Ed has no problem with motivation. His motivation is always to escape from Leatherface. I, however, need more details. I make inquiries:

ME: So, Ollie. The Assassination. Did I do it?

OLLIE: I have no f——g idea.

ME: Well, it kind of seems like the FBI may be part of some big conspiracy here, don't you think?

OLLIE: This interrogation is part of the public record. What was the FBI up to? No one really knows. You decide.

ME: Oh. Thanks for the help.

OLLIE: By the way, did you know that you look like Kevin Costner?

ME: Yeah. I get that all the time.

OLLIE: You could be Kevin Costner's evil twin. (Note: In case you forgot, Costner plays attorney Jim Garrison in the movie.) You know, by the end of the case, Jim Garrison was so paranoid he was checking his own children's fingerprints every morning to make sure the CIA hadn't replaced them with look-a-like midget secret agents. Maybe we could work that angle with *you*.

ME: Yeah! Yeah! That's the ticket! I could be

	the anti-Costner! That's brilliant, Ollie! Just brilliant!
OLLIE:	Of course, that would mean Jim Garrison would be checking his own fingerprints.
ME:	Evil twin! Evil twin!
OLLIE:	(*Musing*) I don't know how that would work.
ME:	Anti-Costner! Anti-Costner!
OLLIE:	Oh hell, I've already got forty-three conspiracy theories in this film. Let's just do the scene.
ME:	(*humping his leg*) Evil twin? Anti-Costner?
OLLIE:	ROLL IT!

We shoot the scene. I decide that my motivation is to save J. Edgar Hoover from the Mafia before they release photos of him in drag.

Next time you rent *JFK*, watch for that.

Squinting with Clint

WHEN IT COMES TO AUDITIONS, Clint Eastwood is another color of fish. Unlike Oliver Stone and other carnivores, with Clint the whole audition process is extremely nonconfrontational. That's because Clint is not there.

Clint Eastwood is so empathetic with actors that he dares not actually watch their auditions in person lest he hire *everybody*. His heart bleeds for the poor actors. What a guy! So what he does is just have his casting director put us on tape and he picks out his actors that way.

The first time I meet him is on the set. He walks up to me and sticks out his hand and says, 'Hi. I'm Clint.' I would have never guessed. 'Anybody ever tell you that you look like Kevin Costner?'

I know what you're saying. *Another* Kevin Costner movie? Yup. I'm caught in a karmic tidepool. A Costner warp. I am folding space back in on itself. I am building a career as a shadowy lookalike making brief appearances in every movie Costner does.

This one is called *A Perfect World*, and it stars Kevin as an escaped convict who kidnaps a boy as a hostage and tries to get to Alaska before the crusty Ranger, played by you know who, catches up with him. They all bond by the third act. It's a bondage flick.

Unfortunately in this case it's not exactly an asset to resemble the Good Twin too markedly. I play a highway patrolman at a roadblock and they don't want any doppelgangers.

Kevin and his hostage have been picked up hitchhiking by a family in a station wagon. (Actually, the father is played by my old Austin acting buddy, John Jackson. John went off to LA-LA and has done quite well. He's about to do much better. Not too long after *A Perfect World* John will get a lead in the military law series *JAG*.) They're in the back with about five other kids, and I stick my head in the window and check out the wagon and there's a moment — a high suspense, critical moment — when I could end the movie thirty minutes early.

But then, clearly enunciating every phonic of my three-word line, I say '*Drive careful, folks*'. And the saga continues.

I've pulled my hat down and Kevin doesn't recognize me. Or else he does but doesn't want to admit it. For a few minutes I am oddly miffed at this. After all, we once danced together. But I'm being too hard on the guy. In the first place *Fandango* has receded in his rearview mirror by now. In the second place Kevin Costner is a *really* big star and has just finished dancing with *Wolves*. In the third place this Highway Patrolman role is not exactly one to fixate the attention. I let it go.

Kevin and Clint seem to enjoy a pretty good relationship. Kevin spends a lot of time pumping the older star for director tricks. (Clint just won the Academy Award for *Unforgiven*.) But Clint spends most of *his* time playing on the railroad tracks with the show's child actor. They're busy over there throwing rocks while everybody else is setting up for the next scene.

When all is ready, Clint kind of lopes over and gives a laconic wave of the hand and we shoot the scene. I am amazed that almost everything is done in one take. I guess Clint has worked with this same crew for years and years and they know exactly what he wants and how to get it. He just doesn't waste time.

For instance: We all pile into vans and go cruising through the backcountry, shooting a car scene. When you see people talking in a car in a movie and driving around with all this scenery in the background, what's usually happening is that they have the car on a trailer behind a truck with the camera on it.

That's the kind of scene we're doing with Kevin and the kid.

There's lots of dialogue as the car speeds over hill and dale. Consequently the cameraman is shooting it all very carefully. After they cut, Clint asks him, 'Did you get it?' And of course the cameraman knows that if he says yes, the shoot is over. That will be *it*. Clint will turn around and go home with only one take in the can.

I guarantee you ninety-nine directors out of a hundred would shoot that rather demanding sequence over and over to make sure they had plenty of coverage. But Clint likes what the actors did and trusts his crew. So the cameraman swallows and says 'Yeah. I think I got it.' Back to base camp.

And that's why Clint Eastwood never goes over budget.

Clint wants to shoot an extra scene with me that's not in the script. Great!

The script calls for Kevin to steal the family's station wagon after making it past Checkpoint Charlie. This leaves the unhappy campers on foot. They have to come trudging back over the hill, like shorn sheep with suitcases. Clint's idea is for me to do a comic take when I first glimpse this parade returning to my roadblock.

No problem. Except that John Jackson and the actors playing the family have left for the day. This does not faze Clint. 'Just look over there and pretend you see them coming over the hill with all their bags. It's gonna be a close-up on you anyway.'

I nod in agreement; I like close-ups on 'me anyway'. But I turn aside as Clint busies himself with the cameraman, a perplexed expression beneath my hat. To follow the director's instructions in this case may seem easy to the uninitiated. But to the true Method Machine like myself, a moment like this is anathema. He has told me to look at *nothing* and *pretend* to see *something*.

The Method school of acting has Basic Tenets. One of them says *never pretend to see something*. The reasoning, in condensed form, is that you need something (real) to focus on, or you might exaggerate (your expression) to compensate for the (nothing). Infringe on this law at your peril. What if another Method actor catches you? You are drummed out of the corps, that's what.

I almost ask if I can have a couple of grips walk over the hill toward me so I can remain true to the Method bible. But something stops me. This is Clint Eastwood and he's in a hurry. He doesn't waste any extra time on great big complicated car-dialogue scenes. So why should he waste time on a highway patrolman who can't react to nothing.

I decide to keep my Method to myself and fake it.

But then I get an inspiration. I take my position. I assume my stance. When the cameras roll, I do not move a muscle. I do not double-take. I simply gaze across the empty landscape and *squint*.

I do an Eastwood squint. And in my head I'm hearing that harmonica from *A Fistful of Dollars* . . .

'Cut! Loved it! Moving on!'

They have a van ready to drive us back to base camp. Kevin Costner and I are the only passengers. I get in the back and Kevin gets in the front and the driver goes off somewhere to check with the assistant director. So it's just the two of us in the car.

It's obvious that Kevin doesn't want to have conversation just now. I respect the silence. But it's weird sitting together in a van and not exchanging even a word. Especially after we just did a scene together.

This is a symptom of fame. You have to build walls to protect yourself from glamorized glad-handers. I suppose I could say, 'Hi, Kevin. You don't remember me but I've done two movies with you and taught you to dance and now you're a big star and people tell me I look like you!' But it seems invasive. Like I have some legitimate claim on the man's attention. No big deal. Let it go.

The driver comes back.

'You hot back there?' he asks.

'Not too bad,' I reply.

'I'll have the A/C on in a second.'

Just an ordinary, polite exchange between fellow human beings.

Tales of the Texas Triangle

IT'S A STORY AS BIG AS ALL TEXAS!
. . . So have your atlas handy. There's some geography involved here and I wouldn't want you to get confused.

Turn to the map of Texas, which takes up two or three pages of most atlases because it's so durn big.

As you know, Texans are real puffed up about this.

Now find Dallas. It's the one with all the highways running in and out of it. Dallas is the Hub of the West. This makes Dallasites more puffed up than your ordinary Texan.

Dallas is the top point of the Triangle. Now find International Highway 45. It heads out of Dallas going southeast. I-45 is the right side of the Triangle, and it goes straight on down about 240 miles to Houston.

Houston is the bottom right point of the Triangle. Houston is the biggest city in Texas, so Houstonians are even more puffed up than Dallasites.

Now you're going to find I-10 heading west from Houston. That's the bottom of the Triangle, and it rambles 180 miles to San Antonio.

San Antonio is the only laid-back city in Texas, and San Antonians don't bother to get all puffed up about anything. However, the Alamo is in San Antonio, so they're quietly smug.

Now that you're in San Antonio you've got to find I-35 heading northeast. It's 280 miles back to Dallas, and eighty miles up is Austin.

Austin is the capital of Texas and is therefore by far the most important place in the whole state.

And if that's not enough, I live there.

Actors in New York may have to work the five boroughs. (Big deal. So you have to buy a lot of subway tokens.)

L.A. actors may have to drive from Santa Monica to the Valley. (My heart bleeds.)

But to make a living in Texas, I have to have an agent in Dallas, Houston, San Antonio and Austin and be ready to drive to whichever city I have an audition or job in.

Don't talk about flying. Sometimes if I get hired on a big movie or television show they'll fly me in, but only in direst need would I fly to an audition. A lot of the jobs I get don't pay enough to cover the cost of a round-trip ticket.

No, to make a living as an actor in this state, you gotta be a long-haul trucker.

Now this here's a little yarn about my early days in the business, when I was young and witlessly optimistic.

It's about the ultimate auditioning challenge: four cities in one day and the terrible consequences thereof.

So put the atlas on the side table and get comfortable. Have yourself some seltzer water or something.

It's a long ride.

Jed's station wagon is full of crap. Not only is the floor knee deep in newspapers, foam cups and ancient burritos, but he's got all these cardboard boxes lined up on the backseat. They're full of headshots and video demo tapes. Then there're the hangers full of suits and khakis and polo shirts.

Jed is a professional actor, and he travels fully armed for any potential employment opportunity, as do I. All my crap is in here too.

It's six o'clock in the morning and Jed and I are on the first leg of an actor's odyssey.

Our desperate plan is to make a 9:30 audition in Dallas, followed by a 10:00. Then we drive like frightened buffalo down I-45 to Houston in order to make two more auditions: a 2:30 and a 3:00.

Forsaking all logic and traffic laws, we then plan to arrive in San Antonio in time for a 6:00 capper.

Following the San Antonio audition, we merely have to countermand the physical limitations of the internal combustion engine and get back to Austin in time for an 8:00 performance of *Streetcar Named Desire*.

We're not *attending* the play; we're *in* it.

There is a well-documented but officially unrecognized scientific principal that applies to TV and film actors: you will only be in demand if you book a vacation or get cast in a play.

My answering machine has been empty for weeks until I agree to be a last-minute replacement down at Center Stage on Austin's infamous Sixth Street.

I'm playing Steve, the upstairs neighbor.

Tennessee Williams severely underwrote this part, but I just played the lead in the last Center Stage production and it seems gracious to help them out. Besides, it's a great play and I get to be in that cool fight scene at the poker game.

Furthermore, you can make literally *hundreds* of dollars a year doing plays.

But now the fickle audition gods are smiling and high-dollar TV and film projects are starting up all over the state. I'm stuck.

Like I said, Jed's in the play too. He plays Mitch. Jed has the same problem as me. He loves theater, but he makes his living as an on-camera actor. He really needs to go to auditions when they come up. But . . . no understudy.

Streetcar could get along without me for a night, but they'd have to cancel if Jed didn't make curtain.

No sweat. We'll make it back. Our itinerary has been impeccably arranged. What could go wrong?

Jed is much higher up the acting rungs than I am. He was actually in L.A. for a while but had to come back to Texas because of an illness in his family. I'm just getting started in the media side of the profession. Jed has done hundreds of jobs.

He's taught me all kinds of stuff about the business: what kind of headshot to have, what to put on a video demo tape, how to kiss agent ass, how to kiss casting director ass, how to kiss film, commercial and industrial director ass . . .

If the acting profession was arranged into grades, like high school, Jed would be a graduate student and I'd be a sophomore.

As we hurtle northward, we remark upon another little known but irrefutable scientific acting fact: if more than one audition/job is involved, everybody will want you on the same day, if not the same hour.

Jed and I have somehow finessed our call times so this will work, but if our audition efforts are successful and we are actually cast in one of these projects in one city or another, our scheduling nightmares will just be beginning.

I am pumping Jed for advice as we traverse the prairies of central Texas.

I have just recently tried to broaden my opportunities by procuring a Dallas agent. This gatekeeper to my destiny is a woman who signed me up but has shown little enthusiasm for my potential.

Actors are needy little beasts. We crave encouragement. When we get a job, we need our agent to pat us on the back and tell us how great we are. When we *don't* get a job, even more so.

We realize that our insatiable appetite for approval becomes tedious, if not obnoxious, but we work in a profession where the best of us are successful only once out of every fifteen or twenty times that we apply for a job, and the average job will usually last one day.

Constant rejection has rendered us pathological.

I tell Jed that my Dallas agent displays few nurturing instincts. In fact, I think she has gone mad.

Last week when I stopped by the agency to drop off headshots, I stuck said head in the door to say 'Hi', and she started yelling,

'Don't talk to me! Don't talk to me!'

Then the other day I was speaking to the receptionist

and a mere glance at my agent through the glass wall of her office was enough to incur the wrath:

'Why are you looking at me?! Why are you looking at me?!'

But that's not the clincher.

Someone has just related to me that my agent uses me as a bad example in the introductory lecture of her career seminar for new talent.

According to reports, she relates an anecdote about one of my visits to her office. In her story I am talking to her and she decides to test my powers of observation by slowly sliding down in her chair, getting shorter and shorter behind her desk. She maintains that I never notice a thing. Therefore I'll never make it as an actor.

How was I to know she wasn't being slowly sucked down the throat of a giant lizard hidden under her desk?

I wouldn't want to interfere with something like that.

Jed suggests I seek new representation immediately.

Dallas comes over the horizon like a smoggy Oz.

If we can negotiate the last vestiges of rush-hour traffic, we should just make it to our first audition on time.

We're going to a swanky hotel to read for a part on *Dallas*.

Jed and I are auditioning for the same part. We didn't get an audition script (called 'sides') in advance, but we know we're supposed to be some sort of Westerner, so we've got our jeans and boots on.

The audition room is on the mezzanine level of the hotel, and ten other guys in jeans and boots are sitting there waiting their turn when we arrive. Jed and I can't afford to wait, so we spend some time politicking with our fellow actors to let us move up in line.

I know most of these guys. A couple of them are from Austin: John Jackson and Mitch Pileggi. Everybody thinks they're brothers because they're both big studly bald guys.

John and Mitch commute for auditions and jobs like I do, but they got smart and went in on a Dallas apartment with two other actors. They just had a good night's sleep while Jed and I are shaking off road-jangle.

We're pals and everything, but these boys are tough to compete against. They've got the looks and they've got the chops. (Luckily for the rest of us, they will soon depart for California and eventual stardom . . . John is now on *JAG* and Mitch on *X-Files*.)

It's my turn. The casting director is named Rody Kent and she's great. Reads well. Supportive. Roots for everybody. Winks at you after the scene when you did it right.

This is not much of a part. A vengeful cowboy with one good line. Something like:

'*I'll get you, J.R., and your little dog too!*'

I does me bit. Rody winks.

The director wants to know if I'm from New York. Well that blows. If he thinks I'm from New York he's not going to cast me as a Westerner.

It's my name. Everybody thinks all Italians are from New York. It doesn't matter that I'm third-generation Texan and used to work on a ranch and rope dogies and three of my grandparents were named Drake, Winstead and Buchanan.

One great-grandfather from Palermo and they'll never let you on a horse.

If I changed my name to Bucky Buchanan I'd score

cowboy parts. It has nothing to do with acting ability, I tell myself. It's all about projecting the right image.

Of course my theory is shot to hell if Mitch Pileggi gets the part. (And he does.) But at least his *first* name sounds Anglo-Saxon.

Bucky Perella?

Hell-bent for leather, Jed and I are back in the saddle. We're already twenty minutes late for our ten o'clock. We do a rush change into our business suits in the parking lot.

This is a commercial audition for a new airline. Southwest is trying out a new luxury commuter line between Dallas and Houston called Muse Air, catering to the executive class.

They've decided that executives resent having to sit next to the unwashed masses on Southwest's regular planes, where everybody flies coach. Executives want to feel pampered and special and superior, but they still don't want to pay TWA prices, so Herb Kelleher has invented a new airline for them.

This is another one-liner. All we have to do is look happily into the camera and say:

'*You can't describe it! You just gotta fly it!*'

Jed goes first and he's out of there in thirty seconds.

I go in. I give the casting director my headshot and she hands it to the director.

'So. You from New York?'

Oh boy . . . But wait a minute. He's smiling.

They've hired a New York ad agency to do this spot and they're a bunch of Italians!

'*Paisan!*'

I'm milkin' it now, baby! I'm giving them the secret

handshake and doing that thing with the eyebrows. I'm telling them about Uncle Guido and singing a chorus of 'Volare'.

The actual audition is a mere formality.

Unless Mitch Pileggi shows up, I'm in.

I-45 in the rain.

It's my turn to drive and we've hit a thunderstorm. We are, predictably, behind schedule. I should be reducing speed in this weather, but fool that I am, making an audition on time is more important than survival itself.

I'm keeping it right at the edge of hydroplane as we blast through the spray that bounces off the mud flaps of the semis we're passing.

Jed and I are still in our dress shirts and suit pants and the humidity inside the car has steamed us up. We're much too late to stop and change.

There's nothing like the smell of wet tweed in the morning.

Our next audition is for a soap opera on the Playboy Channel. Our Houston agent has instructed us to wear something 'decadently casual'. (This should have been a clue as to the nature of the audition, but our hunger for employment has rendered us oblivious to subtleties.)

We exit the freeway into downtown Houston at 2:45. We're already fifteen minutes late and we're supposed to be at the second audition by three. There's no option but the Chinese fire-drill.

At the first red light we're ready. We've cased the street for cops and have our casual slacks in our laps. *Go!*

Jed and I jump out of the car in the middle of the

stopped traffic and with car doors open remove our suit pants and soaked shirts. The Houston drivers around us take in the free show with high good humor and give us appreciative honks. We bounce into our slacks and button up our decadently casual shirts and we're back in the car in time for the light change.

A jaunty wave to our new fans and we're off.

Talk about road-jangle. We've just driven 440 miles with one stop for a couple of auditions. Our pancreases have been on stop/start, producing the adrenaline required for fight-or-flight responses to casting directors and diesel semis in the rain.

We've had nothing but coffee since six and we need to go to the bathroom.

It's time to get sexy.

The Playboy Channel is looking for beautiful people to put in hot tubs on late-night television.

The audition scene is something about a guy with his best friend's wife. She gets something in her eye. (There's an original plot device for you!) While attempting to aid her, the guy is overcome with eyelid lust and starts desperately tonguing her eye socket.

Somewhere, a saxophone starts playing.

The casting director is living a dream.

When I enter the audition room he's sitting in his peacock chair surrounded by actresses. The first reading for the woman's role has been completed, and these are the chosen ones who have been asked to remain for the callback.

It is obvious that Jed and I have not exactly pushed the envelope of decadently casual, wardrobe-wise.

The casting director has not been able to let these beauties out of his sight. He's decided to let them stay in the room with him while he reads the men. They're draped all over his chair and edging each other aside in their efforts to get closer to the Man.

The Source of All Things Hollywood. The Font of Fame. The Wellspring of Castability. *El Jefe Grande.*

I have entered a casting seraglio.

Trying to keep a straight face, I attempt a reading. Upon completion, *El Jefe* informs me that he will announce who is to be called back after all the men have auditioned. I am expected to wait. I very politely mention that I have another audition. 'Is there any way to find out sooner?'

'I'll make it easy for you,' he says. 'If you can't wait, then you're not called back. Next!'

Looking back on these things, it's easy to imagine myself responding heroically. Why didn't I come up with a bitingly witty rejoinder, like:

'You know what *you* are? You're just a big *Pooper!* That's what *you* are!'

Then I could have thrown the nearest starlet over my shoulder in a fireman's carry and made a dignified exit.

Alas, the stark truth is, I slither out of there on my belly like an eel-boy, leaving only the embarrassed twitters of the harem in my wake.

I tip Jed off on what to expect. Since we are already late for the second audition, we decide to split up. Jed will roll the dice on the Playboy thing while I go to the next appointment. Then I'll come back for him and we'll hie on to San Antonio.

When I show up at the next casting session the waiting room is empty. I have changed back into my clammy suit for naught. The whole thing is over. I poke my head into the room and see them packing up the video equipment.

'Sorry to be late. Unavoidably detained . . . rabid harem girls . . . wild dogs ripping at my innards . . .' etc. etc.

The director takes pity on me. His name is Jay and he's a decent sort . . . for a director. He unpacks the camera and let's me audition.

The job is an industrial training film for Exxon. The script is about 'harnessing computing power' and other fascinating activities of the corporate life.

At this point in the day I am so brain-fried that I give a completely natural and blank-faced rendition of an engineer who knows absolutely nothing about his new computer system.

I am perfect for the part.

Serendipitous irony. Jay and I will be buddies for the next fifteen years.

I have picked Jed up and we are negotiating the bottom side of the Triangle on I-10. All is not well with my friend.

I take it things did not go splendidly at the Playboy mansion.

Jed makes me pull into a 7-Eleven where he purchases a six-pack to dull the pain. After slamming home a couple of Miller's finest, he tells me the sad tale.

He made the callback all right.

The thing was, the callback consisted of stripping down to your shorts and displaying your body for the purpose of determining if you were hot tub-worthy.

Making a surprise appearance in your skivvies in front of anonymous motorists at a red light is one thing. Shedding your tweeds for the Casting God and his goddess girls is another. But Jed went through with it.

Jed has a decent physique. He boxes to stay in shape and used to be a star quarterback before acting became more of a buzz than sports. (He can still throw a pass sixty yards downfield.)

The problem seems to have been that Jed was wearing his white Jockey briefs today. And after 440 miles glued to a sweaty car seat they were in less than immaculate condition.

It takes two more beers before he can get philosophical about it.

We are wandering around San Antonio, the charming Alamo City.

When the early Spanish settlers started a mission here, they let their cows wander hither and thither, yinder and yonder. Then later, wherever the cows made a wide enough path, they called it a street. Still later, it was arbitrarily decided that most of these streets would be one-way, for no discernible reason. (I think so that everybody would get a good long look at the Alamo, because that's where you always end up after you keep turning on all the one-way streets.)

I'm driving. Jed is no help at all, by now. He's been unconscious for the last hundred miles. He keeps slumping over the gearshift and I have to push him aside. He's drooled all over himself and he reeks of stale beer.

It's bad for my morale to see my mentor in this condition. After I finally find the right one-way street to turn down and we disembark at the audition, I slap Jed around and give him a pep talk.

'You can do it! Get in there and fight! This is an industrial audition . . . the odds are good that they won't want us to undress!'

Jed goes to the bathroom to clean up while I take my turn in the audition room.

Having just been successful with my corporate zombie technique at the Exxon thing, I try it again. Except this time the character is a spokesman who's supposed to know what all the incomprehensible acronyms stand for as he speaks confidently into the camera lens:

'Here at Hydrogenated Veeblefetzer International, we stand behind our MFPs. Thanks to charcoal activation, our VORT-mongers are both CROM-data and DRG-5 compatible. We skip the light fandango and turn cartwheels cross the floor. We shop at A & P and the crowd calls out for more.'

I go through it twice, but it doesn't get any better.

Jed is up. He's been in the bathroom, practicing the script. He's oh-for-four today and he knows it. One last shot.

He enters the room. My fellow auditionees and I can hear his performance through the closed door. I don't think Jed even makes it through the first Veeblefetzer before he starts laughing. Actually they're *all* laughing. It's a spontaneous outburst of jocularity cascading forth from the audition cell.

After order is restored, Jed gives it another whirl. This time he goes all the way through, word perfect. Applause! My God! He's getting *applause* for his reading!

Jed comes out, followed by the whole room full of writers, directors, cameramen and corporate flacks. They're pounding him on the back and beaming at him as they bid him a fond farewell. Their Golden Boy.

The new corporate spokesman of Hydrogenated Veeblefetzer International.

As we sample cow tracks in search of a freeway on-ramp, Jed clues me in on his devastating technique.

He knows that everybody is getting two run-throughs of the difficult script. He also knows that all the other guys who have gone in there, (including me) have been grim and determined and nervous about screwing up.

So Jed, cagey veteran that he is, intentionally garbles the first sentence and collapses in uncontrolled, self-deprecating laughter. This is infectious, and soon everybody in the room is cracking up, charmed and entertained by his buffoonery. They've had a long day of watching actors struggle painfully with those deadly acronyms, and they've probably been restraining their mirth out of common decency.

Jed has given the auditioners a much-needed release. He also knows, with an actor's sense of psychology, that there is almost nothing as attractive and endearing as the sight of someone laughing gleefully at his own folly.

And then he nails the second take, giving them the opportunity to reward him for bringing light into their drab industrial day.

Touché!

And to think I was starting to feel sorry for the wily devil.

Home sweet I-35. How comforting to be breaking the speed limit on our very own neighborhood interstate.

We make Austin and pull up to the stage door in the alley behind Center Stage at 7:55.

Jed and I cannot help but acknowledge the cosmic significance of this. We have thrown ourselves on to the winds of our actors' karma and come wafting back to earth, justified.

And here is our theater, ready to redeem us from the crass prostitution of network soap and corporate dogma flogging. Here to greet and enfold us like a comforting womb of acting purity.

The haggard stage manager is at the door:

'Where the hell have you jerk-offs been?'

EPILOGUE

Jed scores big on the Veeblefetzer thing: three days of work at narrator rate.

I get hired on the Exxon industrial and the Muse Air commercial, but they schedule them on consecutive days. I drive to Houston and sleep on Director Jay's floor, where I catch a hideous cold. I take antihistamines for the cold and lose my voice. Half way through filming the next day I am reduced to a ghastly whisper.

Jay very nicely postpones work until the next day. Then I inform him that I have to go to Dallas for the commercial. I volunteer to return and complete the project for free at a later date.

I spend all night in a bathtub at the Holiday Inn, trying to loosen up my voice enough to do one line in the commercial, which may be worth $10,000 to me. My Dallas agent informs me that even though my call time in Dallas is not until evening, they want me in town by ten or else. She has another talent standing by if I can't regain my voice.

I have to buy a round-trip airplane ticket to Dallas. When I get there I hire a cab to drive me to the nearest doctor's office. I pay another $70 to get a cortisone shot in my neck. This improves my voice barely enough to hang on to the job.

With no sleep for thirty-six hours and pneumonia setting in, I dress up in my peppy little executive suit and smile into the camera and say,

'You can't describe it. You just gotta fly it!' with just enough timbre and resonance to please my Italian employers.

I fly back to Houston, retrieve my car, and drive to Austin where I remain sick in bed for a week.

Muse Air folds within the year.

Derailing *Streetcar*

THE CAST OF OUR PRODUCTION of *Streetcar Named Desire* is a little inbred.

The actors playing Stanley and Stella are married. That works as long as they're getting along. But what if some night they're experiencing marital strife, and Stanley is yelling, 'Stella! Stella!' and she looks down and says 'Fuck you, Asshole!'?

Our Stanley is famous for two things:

First of all, he used to be a gymnast and can walk around on his hands for half an hour. He likes to do this in the middle of rehearsals.

Stanley's second claim to fame is his penchant for onstage practical jokes.

I remember an epic moment in a production of *The Odyssey*. This was a play for children that traveled around to elementary schools.

The play is being performed in the gymnasium of one of these schools and Stanley is playing Ulysses. Stanley is standing at the mast, as the ship, tempest-tossed, struggles through the waves. (They've got a little cardboard ship that the other actors are pretending to row.) Stanley starts improvising lines while exhorting his men to row more fervently, and he comes up with this gem:

'*Hard on, men! Stroke! Stroke!*'
I'm not sure if he followed this with a handstand.

The actress playing Blanche DuBois is living with the director. This is bad. That's because every actress who plays this part, the most famous role in American theater, goes insane.

Jessica Tandy took to beating up Marlon Brando on stage. Vivian Leigh? 'Nuff said. Ann-Margret admits that the part nearly drove her over the edge.

Not to flaunt tradition, our Blanche is bonkers. She's gone Method and is hitting the mint juleps for the purpose of character identification. She's a fine actress and is holding it up on stage, but all is not rosy-peachy-keeno on the homefront.

Our director is subconsciously acting out by devising more and more abusive blocking for his star girlfriend. He's practically got Stanley dragging her around by the hair. Even more worrisome: I think Blanche *likes* it.

For me, doing *Streetcar* is the first time I get to relax all day. I'm playing Steve, the upstairs neighbor, who has almost nothing to do except the poker game. That's good, since my fellow road warrior, Jed, and I have just returned from a near circumnavigation of the state of Texas in search of media employment. Best of all, I get to stop looking cute for corporate America. I put on my grubby costume and color in the space between my eyebrows with satisfaction.

Jed is, like I said, playing Mitch. That's a big part and he's got to keep it together. I'll keep an eye on him; he's looking a bit logy.

As you must remember, *Streetcar* is set in New Orleans in the French Quarter. Stanley and Stella live in the bottom apartment of a two-story, under Steve and his wife, Eunice. There's supposed to be an outside staircase as part of the set.

Coincidentally, Center Stage has a staircase right in the middle of the upstage area. It's an old theatre, and because of limited space, the dressing rooms are upstairs, over the stage. Actors who are not onstage can keep track of the play by looking down through cracks in the old wooden floor.

Our set designer incorporates this whole arrangement into the set, making the dressing room double as Steve and Eunice's apartment.

At one point, Stanley and Stella are supposed to listen to Steve and Eunice make love upstairs. Everybody in the dressing room loves this part because they get to watch Eunice and me pant and moan and make bumping noises on the wood floor.

Everybody except Jed. That's because the actress playing Eunice is his brother's fiancée.

Like I said . . . inbred.

Everything goes well until the poker game fight.

Our stage manager has gotten surly with the men of the cast because we keep destroying the set every night. We've been indulging ourselves by splintering chairs and wrecking the table. We also spill beer and food and cards all over the stage and then drag Stanley through it.

At the end of the fight we're supposed to cool Stanley down in the shower. They've set up a real working shower onstage and we're taking full advantage. All that water mixed with the rest of the junk makes for a satisfying, slimy stage mulch.

Then we get to watch the actresses slide around for the rest of the night.

Our stage manager thinks we should just kind of shove the table to one side and muss up a chair and be done with it. He's tired of gluing the furniture back together after each performance.

We tell him if he wanted a neat, tidy little fight he should have hired wussy actors.

Real men mulch the stage.

Another interesting factor in all of this is the rake.

Our designer has gotten artsy on us and set the stage at a good fifteen-degree angle towards the audience. Improved sight lines, he says. He doesn't have to walk on it.

Also, things tend to roll offstage into the audience.

So here we are having the fight. We've smashed a bunch of stuff, as usual. Jed and I are really into it tonight, probably because we've been trapped in a car all day and need the exercise.

The table has been turned over, and all of a sudden one of the beer bottles starts to roll down the stage and into the first row.

This has happened before and we like it. It's somehow hypnotizing. We all stop fighting and watch, stupidly, in a frozen tableau, as the longneck disappears over the edge of the stage with a satisfying crash. The audience laughs. We start fighting again.

Stanley sees another bottle at his feet. He kind of gently nudges it with his foot and *it* starts rolling downhill. Again we all stop struggling so we can enjoy the spectacle as it obeys the call of gravity and picks up speed on its way to a glassy death.

Crash!

The audience cheers this time. Cue the fight.

So now we're all looking around for more bottles to satisfy the audience's lust for destruction. As each new missile hurtles downhill, the crowd yells,

'Timber!' and, 'Look out below!'

(All except the patrons in the first row, who are busy dodging broken glass.)

It might not be what Tennessee Williams had in mind.

Finally we throw Stanley into the shower and, having thoroughly goobered up the set, retreat up the stairs to the dressing room while he starts yelling for Stella.

We're all chuckling as we dry off. After a while we dimly perceive that a silence is now engulfing the stage. Eunice looks through the cracks in the floor. She reports that Blanche is walking around down there not saying anything.

'Wait a minute,' says Eunice. 'Aren't *you* supposed to be in this scene?'

She's pointing at Jed, who is sitting there with his pants off. With an electric shock of sudden coherence, he squeals, 'Oh my God!' and dives down the staircase, trying to get his pants back on as he descends.

After the poker fight, Mitch is supposed to get lovey-dovey with Blanche. Jed has short-circuited and started changing for Act Two.

This has left Blanche with nothing to do but wander around the stage, a lonesome Southern belle.

Jed comes tumbling down the stairs with his pants around his ankles.

Blanche has been looking languorously out at the audience, and hearing the rumpus, assumes her Mitch has finally decided to appear. She turns and prepares to begin the scene.

But her Mitch is not there. He is hiding behind the stairs, trying to fix his zipper.

The dead air is deafening.

Finally, Jed decides to start the dialogue from behind the stairs, hoping that he'll get his zipper up at some point in the scene.

'*Pssttt! . . . Miss DuBois!*'

Blanche doesn't respond to her invisible suitor, so Jed tries to get her attention with a little adlibbing:

'*Over here! Under the stairs! I got somethin' I wanna show ya!*'

Jed peaks around the corner of the stairs, giving her and the audience a little flash of underpants.

Some days it's all about underpants.

Blanche comes up with a line from the script that has relevance to the present situation:

'*I'm terrified!*'

Jed thinks they're back on script:

'*Ho-ho! There's nothing to be scared of . . .*'

Blanche slightly alters a line:

'*But you're not properly dressed!*'

Jed dutifully picks up the cue:

'*That don't make no difference in the Quarter!*'

The audience is really into it now. This is the most entertaining performance of *Streetcar Named Desire* they've ever seen. It's one of those magic nights when truly special things happen.

As is often the case when the wheels start coming off, the actors get maniacally energized and start trying too hard to redeem themselves.

Jed and Blanche are doing the paper lantern scene, where Mitch tries to get a good look at Blanche so he can tell how old she is.

Like everything else on our set, the Japanese paper lantern has seen better days. Jed tears it down off the bare light bulb every night and the stage manager, who is trying to save money on this shoestring production, tapes and glues it back together. The lantern is one of those cheap, ribbed things; thin yellow paper stretched over a wire spiral frame. By this time the wire has come unhinged and is hanging out the bottom of the paper.

So here comes the moment:

'. . . *I've never had a real good look at you, Blanche. Let's turn the light on here.*'

Blanche: '*Light? Which light? What for?*'

Mitch: '*This one with the paper thing on it.*'

Jed reaches up to tear the lantern down and grabs a handful of the wire that's hanging out the bottom. When he pulls, the wire starts unraveling, leaving the paper part untouched.

Jed now has a spool of wire in his hand, so he takes a mighty swipe with his other hand and makes another attempt to pull the lantern down. Again he misses the paper and grabs nothing but wire.

Now he's got wire wrapped around both hands.

Blanche is watching in helpless fascination.

Jed starts desperately pawing the air, trying to rid himself of this deadly wire. There's a surprising amount of it in these lanterns and it's snaking around him like a giant slinky.

Little pieces of paper and spools of wire are bouncing around the set now while Jed grunts in his efforts to finally destroy the lantern.

Blanche has moved upstage, out of harm's way.

The audience is enraptured.

Finally Jed, with a furious howl, launches himself at the light bulb itself and rips the whole electrical socket down from the roof of the set.

Jed and Blanche complete the rest of the scene in ambient light while surrounded by spools of wire. It makes interesting little *sproing-sproing* noises when they kick it with their feet.

We're on a roll now.

The light board operator has had to adjust the lights to compensate for Jed tearing down the light bulb in the previous scene. He's rattled.

It's the climax of the play, when Stanley picks up drunken, crazy Blanche and carries her off to the bedroom while delivering his famous '. . . *We've had this date with each other from the beginning!*' line.

Stanley slings her up and prepares to exit upstage to the bedroom. But the light guy hits the lights too early and blacks out the stage. Now Stanley has to negotiate the exit in pitch darkness, through mounds of stage mulch and coils of wire, while using Blanche's head as a battering ram.

The audience can't see anything, but they can hear a lot.

'*Clip-clop* . . . *sproing sproing* . . . *Thud!* Ouch! Shit! . . .

sproing sproing . . . splash Thud! Ouch! Jesus! . . . *sproing sproing sproing . . .*'

At curtain call, Blanche comes out with a bandaged head, Jed drops a beer bottle into the pit, Stanley stands on his hands and Eunice and I pick up slinky wire and twirl it around like pompoms while we pant and moan and stomp our feet.

I think this is the only night we get a standing ovation.

Center Stage goes broke and our director closes it down and moves to England. Blanche eventually goes to rehab. Jed gets cast in *Jaws III*. Stanley and Stella stay married (for a while) and have a kid.

That winter Stanley and I play Scrooge and Bob Cratchit, respectively, in *A Christmas Carol*. In our first scene at the counting house, I open the ledger and find page after page of *Penthouse* centerfolds pasted therein.

Here we go again.

Smash Cut

SUBTITLE: *'If you're actually going to kill me in this scene I'll need more money up front.'*

I wince involuntarily when the airplane motors start up. The dragon-breath rush of wind through the propellers makes me flinch from blows as yet undealt. It's some other poor fool out there in the dark now, getting his famous self beat to shit. My turn is coming.

The source of my dread anticipation is a battery of three swamp boats parked on trailers with airplane engines mounted on their backs. I hear them revving to a frightful roar, pushing wind at seventy miles per hour toward the backyard of this North Texas country club.

We are making a film noir classic-to-be, as yet unnamed but multistarred. Mary Tyler Moore is in this movie. She's nowhere near these wind machines though. They have been saving that treat for us lesser, expendable lights. Except for James Coburn and Eric Stoltz. But at least they get the big money. I've been lowballed into doing this epic for near scale. I thought January would be slow.

It turned out to be cold. Especially at one in the morning when we're shooting these scenes. A week of cold, tired, special-effects, movie-glamour hell. All night every night until the subsidiary characters have been killed off and the hero walks alone into the post-tornado dawn, his prostitute-with-a-heart-of-gold girlfriend tucked protectively into his storm-tempered armpit.

There's the second assistant director. I'm called to the set. I zip up my wet suit over two pairs of long johns, put on my business suit costume and cover it all up with a goose down jacket.

I step out into the dark.

Eric Stoltz plays a newspaperman who has come back to his hometown of Tulsa and stumbled into a murder cover-up. Mary Tyler Moore is his mom. Deborah Unger is his high school sweetheart, now married to druggie white-trash James Spader. James Coburn is the town bigshot, and I am Coburn's deviant son. Joanna Going is the prostitute-in-distress. The climax of the movie takes place in a tornado.

The King Bull Daddy Stunt Coordinator is effulgent. He's semi directing these sequences because they're stunts. But not *officially* stunts. Officially they're 'action sequences' for which we actors are to expect no extra compensation.

Bull Daddy hands me a gun and explains my responsibilities in this scene.

I am to come stumbling out of my rich father's house into the teeth of the climactic and highly metaphorical tornado, firing my gun and yelling obscenities at the escaping hero and his damsel. Bull Daddy suggests I stop and reload by the tree.

'I hate it when they never reload, don't you?'

I mention that in the previous scene I had picked up this gun after somebody else dropped it on the floor. Do I just happen to have extra ammo in my coat pocket?

'OK, never mind the reloading. As your reward for saving me from embarrassment, why don't you fall down by the tree and kind of grovel around for a minute?'

The swamp boats are ready. At least the helicopter is on break. Sometimes they use the helicopter to kick up extra dust. (Not cheap, those helos. I can still hear them whining about budget restraints when my agent was negotiating my fee.)

'ACTION!'

I stagger out into a world of fun. I start off in the general direction of my offstage quarry, but it's right into the wind and I can't make much headway. The lights and the smoke they are pumping on to the set blind me. I slit my eyes like a Gobi Mongol against the leaves and sticks and clods that the grips are throwing in front of the propellers to bombard me with in a highly realistic, photogenic and totally tornadic way.

My first take ends when a flying stick bounces off my head. That does the trick. I lurch past the wind machines and collapse.

As they're reloading more blanks in my pistol I kind of casually mention to the grips that maybe they could, ah, you know, like, *glean* the leaf piles of extra sticks and clods so that maybe I won't be scarred for life?

'Well, we did the same thing to Eric and he's the Star.'

I ask them what happens when they blind Eric and they can't finish the movie? They agree to minimal gleaning as long as nobody yells at them. (The constant cry for 'MORE LEAVES!' has already become a catch phrase of the shoot.) Take two.

I enter staggering, once again plaything of the winds. This time, for dramatic variety as well as survival, I grab on to the tree early and cling there as I scream epithets at my retreating enemies. I feel like Heathcliff in *Wuthering Heights*, screaming into the storm for his lost Cathy. On the bright side, no sticks slam into my head at seventy miles per hour and I begin to think this take may do it. No such luck.

'Loved what you did with the tree but we didn't have it in frame. Do it again just like that.' (To grips: 'MORE LEAVES THIS TAKE!')

The engines rev up. Somehow they sound louder. I step around the corner and find out why: They've speeded up the wind to about ninety. I take one dogged step into it and try to find the tree. The wind finds it for me, picking me up and slamming me into the trunk. I kind of flutter there for a few seconds, like a wind sock. My arms and legs are completely useless and I slide down the trunk on to the ground.

Maybe I just can't hear them any more, but nobody seems to be yelling cut, so I crawl toward the camera. I'm having no problem mooding up for the obscenities. I seem to have retained my gun. I fire it in the general direction of the stunt coordinator, wishing they weren't blanks. Wet leaves are blowing into my face so hard that they just stick there.

By the time I have finally clawed my way out of camera range I look like a plant.

Everyone is delighted.

'Oh baby! Oh baby! That's in the *picture*, man! That is *in* the picture! Great job, man! Oh. You hurt? You're all right? OK everybody! Let's do it one more time for safety!'

The night wears on. My fellow thespians and I take turns getting blown to hell. There is a delay while Eric gets a leaf removed from his eye. He has some choice words for the leaf grips.

Finally we're ready for the scene where the scrappy girl Friday jumps on my back just as I'm about to assassinate our hero. She's supposed to claw at my eyes and karate my gun hand until I turn the tables.

First we do the scene with a stuntwoman. She jumps, she claws, I throw her over my shoulder, punch her and kick her in the face. She then rolls off down the hill in the wind. This is my second fight with a woman in this picture and I've won them both. No major damage except a hyperextended elbow from throwing fake punches. After the tree episode I'm not complaining.

Now it's time for the actual Girl Friday actress to come on set and do the close-ups. This is her first time in front of the wind machines. She's a Tony award–winning Broadway musical star named Randy. Welcome to Texas, ma'am, how well do you take a punch?

Randy inhales a leaf on her first take and forgets to claw my eyes or go for the gun or anything. She just kind of clings to my back like a jockey as I rage around in circles pretending to be in deep distress. By the time we get to the face kick, however, Randy's years of theatrical training pay off and she hits the deck like the pro she is.

The problem take is when she is supposed to karate the gun out of my hand in close-up. We can't get it to look real and the director is exasperated with us. Finally they just leave the wind machines on and we pantomime various ways for her to try hitting my arm. Thirty karate blows later I have a very sore forearm and the side of Randy's hand is swollen and numb.

It's finally time for my death scene. Thank God! I have never been so ready to die.

The agent of my demise is the heart-of-gold-prostitute, played by Joanna Going. She's going (yeah, I know) to stick a bowie knife into my spinal column just before I plug Eric Stoltz. I'm supposed to kind of express something with my eyes (the script describes it as a 'nullity'), then fall face forward into the camera. Joanna will be standing horrified but resolute behind me as the camera slowly pans down to show the knife quivering in my terminated carcass.

This technique is called a 'forced reveal' in cinematic terms. It definitely qualifies as an Art Shot, and our French cinematographer is getting excited. You can tell because his English starts to slip as he checks light meters and gives orders to his minions.

'*Non! Non!* Geeve me 40K! 40K! *Merde!* Eeets raining! We are fooked! Fooked!'

This will be my martini shot. When it's over I'll come back to life, go into my trailer and *get warm*. Best of all, I'll be lying on the ground pretending to be dead while Eric and Joanna cling together facing the wrath of the tornado, which is scripted to go 'white out' in its intensity and blow them existentially apart.

They get me into the knife-rigged shirt and I practice my nullities while they set up the shot. I decide on a variation of Oliver Hardy's famous series of takes when Lupe Velez (the Mexican Spitfire) cracked a raw egg down the front of his pants.

It's . . . *there* . . . then it moves to . . . *There* . . . then it oozes on down to . . . *THERE!*

Thank God for the Method. They buy it. We only have to do sixteen takes.

Since this is the climax of the film the brass is rabid.

'More leaves! More smoke! More wind! MORE EVERYTHING! ACT, DAMMIT! ACT!'

After I nullify myself I just close my eyes, and the holocaust doesn't bother me except that it's god-awful cold lying on the ground, even in a wet suit.

But poor Joanna. They've got her in a little black vinyl mini-combo that covers about ten per cent of her starved, ninety-pound movie starlet body. (Hollywood says: 'Looks great on camera though, baby!') A wet suit is not an option and she has mostly frozen. She has to lean against the torrent of air to stand up.

The leaf grips keep improving their technique, and soon Joanna is crying from all the crud in her eyes. They shoot it again and again.

Eric also is a real trouper. (Or a masochist like the rest of us.) Despite being nearly blinded earlier he lets himself get blown repeatedly down the hill. Stardom must be so gratifying.

Entertainment Tonight is doing a segment on us, and after I wrap they come up and interview me.

'You just spent all night getting the crap beat out of you! So how does it *FEEL?!!?*'

My mouth is too cold for words. My nose is running and my hair has been blown into a startled pompadour. The bloody rubber knife is protruding from my back and I'm still spitting out bits of vegetation. But I try to answer their questions for all the fans out there in TV land.

'Well,' I say, 'I guesshth thatth jutht Thyow Bizjshth!'

Tuesday. We wrapped at 7:30 A.M. Now it's sundown and I'm back in the honey wagon (the portable dressing rooms), preparing for another night of abuse.

All the same I am keyed up. Tonight is the big Car Stunt. A few weeks ago the assistant stunt coordinator asked me if I wanted to 'stand near the window when the car drives through it.' Sounded fairly interesting at the time, what with a hinted-at 'stunt bump' to augment my meager salary. Also I had just won my first fight with an actress in the movie and was feeling unusually macho. Anyway I may have – kind of – more or less said yes. Maybe I should have done some research.

They've built a mock-up of the room where the patriarch, James Coburn, delivers his 'seed grass' speech. Our hero, Eric Stoltz, has penetrated the inner sanctum and now denounces me, the spoiled rich-kid, scum-sucking son, as the twisted woman-killer that I happen to be.

By way of response, Famous James looks out the floor-to-ceiling windows of his study onto the rolling lawns of his oil baron estate and gives a botany lesson about the perfect seed grass that he has genetically cultivated. The seed must be preserved from impurities, and likewise I, his beloved son, must be preserved because of the genetic perfection I have inherited from him.

All of this delivered in that remarkably sonorous bass voice that sells stuff on TV all the time.

The upshot is that Daddy is going to save me from impurities by offing Eric instead of turning me in to the cops.

At this point, Joanna Going's stunt double will drive an Austin-Healey through the floor-to-ceiling windows.

As outside the Storm Rages.

Endless hours of set preparation have given me plenty of time to genetically cultivate Angst. I smell a debacle. For whereas stars James and Eric have stand-in stuntmen, Doran and I will be standing in for ourselves. (Doran plays the Tattooed Man, Coburn's henchman and family retainer who, as the car hits, is holding a gun to Eric's head.)

My job is to lean on a couch next to the window and jump out of the way as the car drives by.

I ask, out of mild curiosity, where the car is going to go? They show me a line on the floor about six inches under my foot.

'If all goes well,' they say, 'the car should come through about here and end up about here, give or take a few feet.'

If all goes well?

On the way through they want said automobile to smash a desk. They also ask me, casually, if I would mind tipping a long oak table stacked with Indian pottery into the path of the oncoming vehicle to provide a little extra bang.

'Just be sure you allow yourself time to jump over the couch.'

This provides some food for thought over the next several hours of prep time. I confer with Doran: Since he will be standing downstage of me, so to speak, if I tip the oak table just right the car should propel it into his person as he leaps out of the way.

We decide to ask somebody exactly *how much* that stunt bump in pay will actually amount to.

Meanwhile I develop an interest in the Indian pottery. I

discover that it is real. As in heavy. As in what goes up must come down. Probably on my head.

I really must have a chat with the director. I find him watching gaffers rig lights from the ceiling and other precarious places. He has that *Ben-Hur* look in his eye. You know, just before the chariot race that butchered a couple of stuntmen? I mention, just in passing, that a lot of these props might get relocated around the room a little bit when the car comes in here to park, right?

Big grin. 'Yeah . . . I know! It's gonna be great!' Then to the grips: 'Don't forget the leaves!'

Doran tells me that the assistant stunt coordinator mentioned that we might get $750 for this caper.

What do you mean . . . *'might'*?

I write out a little memo that someone can find on my body so that my widow can be compensated. I ask the assistant stunt coordinator to sign it. He is outraged.

'We won't know how much the stunt is worth until after you do it!'

'What do you mean . . . "*after* I do it"?'

'When we decide how dangerous it really was, then we decide how much to give you.'

'Like hell, you say? You mean you macho sons of guns jump off a building before you even know how much you're going to get?'

'Sure. All the time. It's the stuntman's code!'

'Well, what's the price *range* so to speak?'

'Anywhere from a hundred to a thousand dollars.'

'Well, forget it then, I'm not lettin' a car come through a window at thirty miles an hour aimed precisely at my ass for one hundred dollars.'

Chaos on the set. Directors are consulted. Producers are consulted. *Everybody* is consulted.

I refuse to stand at the couch by my death mark until I receive financial satisfaction.

Finally King Bull Daddy Stunt Coordinator himself approaches me. Famous industry-wide. Worked with the Greats. Knows how to deal with recalcitrant costars. He's the one who wrapped me around the tree last night, but now he shows his diplomatic side.

Bull Daddy gently compliments me on what a good job I did the night before, and explains how he's *making sure* I get an extra $300 to compensate me for windsock duty and leaf burn. 'And this is much more dangerous, so you'll be picking up a nice bonus. We'll figure out exactly how much after we shoot it. I'll take care of you, don't worry!'

I say, well, OK, I trust you. We shake and they rev up the car.

We take our positions. Since the head stuntman is the only one facing the window, we are supposed to cue on him for our respective leaps to safety. But now he says, 'But don't depend on me! Listen to that car hit the wooden ramp. When you hear that, get out of the way quick! Be sure to push that table over!'

I have been mentally mapping out a soft place to land on the other side of the couch. Now I consider placing a few pillows close at hand to put over my head when debris starts falling from above. I remind Doran that the oak table has a date with his spinal column. He nods grimly.

The French cinematographer is yelling last-minute instructions. All eight producers are chewing their lips as they watch their money being spent on this mayhem. The *Entertainment Tonight* boys are here with their TV cameras, and local newspaper reporters are running around doing sideline interviews.

Out there in the mysterious dark, about eighty yards away, the stuntwoman driver is revving up the engine of the red convertible. A chain has been attached to its underside that is supposed to bring the vehicle to a sudden halt just before it can demolish the camera.

As for me, I am philosophical. Calm even. *Red Badge of Courage*, etc. etc. All the same, whatever I'm getting for this is becoming a less and less significant amount of money.

'Start the fans!'

Our old friends the swamp boats now begin their plaintive whine. Plaintive but *loud* . . . and I realize that *hearing* the car hit the wooden ramp will not be a factor. I yell over to the stunt guy: 'How we gonna hear when to . . . ?'

Then I notice his eyes. They just got big. I am still sitting relaxed on the couch, waiting for action. Suddenly I hear someone screaming over the noise of the fans . . .

'Here it comes!'

I jerk my neck toward the window and see headlights. They are bouncing up and down and they are bright. Oh mama!

I do a back somersault over the couch as the car explodes through the wall and passes under my right leg.

I hit the floor already in the fetal position, as blasted objects rain down upon my cowering self. I wait for an Indian pot to skull me.

A yell. Is somebody dead?

Even if they are we are supposed to stay in our positions until the camera has recorded all.

Stillness.

Yahoo! I am not dead and I am a macho stunt stud to boot!

'CUT!'

Cheers! We all stand up, and there is the car. It's a few feet short of the final mark and a few feet to the right. That's because in my consummate professionalism I have tipped the oak table at just the right time, and the Austin-Healey has hit it solid.

As for the table, *it* has hit Doran solid.

Much as we predicted, the oak table was thrust forward at an alarming rate into his hip. Luckily he was padded, but he still has a week's worth of sore ass to look forward to.

The stuntwoman driver is a bit dazed but unhurt. I observe the dent where the fender hit my table. It does not take calculus to figure out what would have happened if I had tipped it over a microsecond later. It would have glanced off the hood and most assuredly penetrated the windshield, possibly decapitating her.

Potsherds are everywhere, but nobody got sherded. The chain didn't break. The car stayed on line mostly. We got lucky in about a dozen ways.

God loves idiots, drunkards and stuntmen.

They let us watch the playback, and there I am, dumbly looking around just in time to haul ass. I decide this is the stupidest thing I've done since I ate those mushrooms with the red dots.

The next night the assistant stunt coordinator comes to see me in my trailer.

'We've decided to give you five hundred bucks, the same as everybody else.'

'OK, if that's the deal. Plus the three hundred dollars for Monday, that's a nice boost . . .'

'No. We're giving you a five hundred dollar bonus for *everything*. The stuff the other night was action sequences, not stunts.'

'How about what King Bull Stunt Daddy said?'

'He's gone back to L.A.'

Luckily I remember somebody once telling me never to punch out a stuntman.

I start climbing into my wet suit and knife-rigged death shirt. Tonight James Coburn gets impaled on his backyard satellite dish. My part consists of continuing to be dead. The shoot is almost over for me. Everyone has been most complimentary about my work. They especially like the way I kill women. Too bad I didn't get to waste Mary Tyler Moore. THAT would have been a feather in my cap.

Maybe they'll use that line I ad-libbed to Eric about 'having his guts on a plate'. Just one magical moment like that can break you out of the pack and put you on the fast track for fame. I remember that Ned Beatty told me that the pig squealing in *Deliverance* was his own idea. Creativity like that does not go unrewarded. Talent will out!

I think on these things as I sit on the edge of my dressing room cot awaiting the call to the set.

I can't lie down because of this knife sticking out of my back.

EPILOGUE

Tornado *(the name ingeniously chosen for this film)*, *is scheduled to come out on the heels of a little movie called* Twister, *which becomes a blockbuster and sets a new standard for digital tornado special effects. A standard which our little film does not come close to reaching.*

The whole tornado plot line is scrapped. Even the car through the window stunt.

I get a call from the producers. They have to bring me out to L.A. to do a new ending for the movie, now called Keys to Tulsa.

Instead of killing me in a tornado they now put me in a confrontation with James Spader and Eric Stoltz and Joanna Going. I get a sweaty close-up and a new death scene.

I also get double my previous salary, a limo ride from the airport, and a suite in one of the best hotels in L.A.

I negotiated that myself.

Guns in the Morning

MY COSTAR SHOT somebody's dick off today. I mean literally. Not a movie dick. A real dick. Off a real person. Not a movie person. In the real world. Not this peculiar hyperspace we call 'Hollywood'.

My costar is a Houston cop, and his day job is being a member of the Houston special elite narcotics squad in charge of chasing down drug dealers and shooting their dicks off. Which he did. Today. In the course of performing his job. He told me all about it just before I shot him in the face.

His movie face, that is. I am not a cop. I do not really shoot people. I am an actor *pretending* to shoot people. That makes it OK. I think.

Black Snow is a Sexy/Action/Drug/Thriller if you're counting genres. It's an independent movie being shot in Houston. To save money on stuntmen, our producers have hired the Houston narco squad to fill in as gang members and drug runners and hit men, since they already know so much about it. Brings that certain authenticity to the screen.

The narco boys are strangely delighted to come in every day after work and shed their plainclothes and perform in our film all night, pretending to be the very street scum they spend all their time trying to arrest. Of course, not all of them can come to the set every night, because sometimes they're out on a caper, but when they *do* show up they bring their own guns.

All of us movie actors are pretending to be hard cases as we brandish our firearms and talk dirty and riddle one another with blanks. We get just a little tenuous when the narcos start talking about their day:

'The guy was naked, see, lying on the bed, when we busted in. He made a move for his gun so I let him have it.'

'Man, you shot him in the hip. It was me that got his dick!'

'Bullshit! Your hand was shaking too much to hit that little old dick of his!'

We movie actors just keep smiling pleasantly as we listen.

Why do these guys want to play cops and robbers with us when they can get the real thing at home, so to speak? It ain't the money, that's for sure. Not on an independent film budget. No, they come down here because they *like* it. These cops are adrenaline junkies. Addicted to violence and its tantalizing proximity. Their main frustration in life is that they don't get to shoot *enough* people's dicks off. And when they do, they have to fill out forms for a week to justify it.

Here in the movies, these cops are expending ammunition in an ecstatic frenzy of slaughter. They get to shoot men, women, gangsters, Colombians, movie stars, and one another. They're in heaven.

Black Snow is a $500,000 movie trying to look like a $5,000,000 movie. Most independent movies can't pull this off. But *Black Snow* does. It rocks. That's because the director is a boy genius named Frank Patterson. He teaches film production at Baylor. Baylor? Yep. That Baptist college in Waco. Frank has himself a tight script with all the requisite sex, drugs and rock 'n' roll. Hardly what you'd expect out of a Baptist education, but there you have it.

Frank has enough money for three weeks of shooting. His secret weapon is his director of photography, Tommy Callaway. This guy works twenty hours a day. He not only shoots every scene, he lights every scene. When he rolls, he gets everything in one take and it looks great.

We are setting some kind of record on this movie. We are cinematically laying rubber through the streets of Houston as we zip through twenty setups a day.

'Take one!'

'That was great! New deal!'

There will be no fine-tuning of the acting instrument. It's strictly seat-of-the-pants time and I love it.

This is the movie that will put me over the top. (If my acting hasn't already). Frank has given me carte blanche to improvise, and that's always dangerous for a man of my propensities.

His first mistake was giving me an ugly shirt. It just does something to me, character-wise, wearing an ugly shirt. Especially when I have a shoulder holster strapped over it.

The plot is kind of hard to explain. It involves a thousand kilos of stolen cocaine in Houston. There's a gang of rednecks led by a drug baron named Coy Harker. I'm his right-hand man, Charlie Balace. I'm a psycho. I talk dirty and wear ugly shirts and I think I'm a cowboy.

Our gang suspects that this other gang has stolen our

product. The other gang is led by somebody called The African, who's from Nairobi and who performs voodoo on chickens. He also makes his men drink his blood to prove their loyalty.

And if that's not enough bad guys for you, the Colombians show up. *Their* leader is named General Ochoa and he wants to know why nobody has paid him for all the cocaine.

These three gangs will be shooting one another for an hour and a half.

The good guys are Travis Winslow, his daughter and his girlfriend. They are innocent people caught up in a situation not of their own making.

Travis's character is defined in one phone call at the beginning of the movie. We see him working out on his home gym when the phone rings:

> Travis: '*Yeah, mac. What does OPEC say. . .? Damn! Eighteen dollars a barrel? I can't pump at eighteen dollars a barrel! . . . Oh well. If I can make it through Khe Sanh I can make it through this . . . Yeah, Jennifer's fine. As well as can be expected for somebody who just lost her mother.*'

That's some efficient exposition, right there.

Travis's teenage daughter is played by Renee O'Connor, who will go to New Zealand and get famous playing *Xena: Warrior Princess*'s sidekick, Gabriella. She spends this movie getting kidnapped by one gang or another.

First Travis takes her out to his old Ranger Dad's house to hide her. Ranger Dad gives Travis his favorite Colt .45 for luck, so right there you know Ranger Dad is a goner.

Sure enough, the African's men grab Renee and leave Ranger Dad bleeding on the throw rug.

So now the African has Renee. But not for long. Just when the African's men start doing the voodoo chicken on her, Travis bursts in and shoots them in a highly choreographed manner with his lucky Colt. But before Travis can escape, the African captures him and wants to pierce his nipple with a weasel bone or something.

Meanwhile, Renee is re-napped by my gun-buddy Dexter and me.

Dexter and I have a Mutt-and-Jeff thing going for a little comic relief. Dexter weighs about three hundred pounds and reads comic books while we're riding around in our black car. I'm always going berserk and throwing his comics out the window while we're shooting people. Hilarity ensues.

The actor who plays Travis doesn't like me. He's from L.A. and he's actually one of the investors in the movie, so Frank kind of had to cast him in the lead. He doesn't like me because in our first scene I beat him severely about the head. (Had to. Scripted, you know.)

Coy Harker sends me over to find out if Travis knows where our dope is. I smash him in the face and knee him in the groin and make lewd comments about his daughter while chewing gum. I guess it's not so much the beating Travis objects to as much as all the new lines I make up. Especially the colorful cuss words I invent on the spot that make the crew laugh.

This is Travis's first scene too, and since he's the lead he was counting on being the bull goose. But I'm young and hungry and born to chew scenery. I have become Nemesis.

Travis gets even more pissed off at me during the car chases.

This being America, all Sexy/Action/Drug/Thrillers are required to have twenty minutes of car chases, minimum. At least one of these must include a car full of bad guys careening around a curve and rolling over just before it hits a hot dog stand. *Black Snow* does not disappoint.

Plus we've got many, many scenes of various bad guys in black cars following other bad guys in black cars and cussing.

It takes time to shoot all these scenes, and a lot of them are at night, so we've set up a semipermanent base camp on an empty corner lot in downtown Houston. All the actors and narco cop stunt men loll around the trailers waiting for our turns behind the wheel of a black car. Mostly we listen to the narco cops tell war stories. There's usually a crowd around the craft services table, listening.

One night a handsome young Hispanic cop is talking about Jamaican drug gangs with Uzis.

It so happens that Director Frank has filled out his crew with interns from his film classes at Baylor. Most of them are starstruck young Baptist women and they have never been in such close proximity to sin. They hang on every lurid description of drug venality that this young cop comes up with. Right now he's talking about marijuana, and how even the cops think it should be legalized, because they don't have time to chase potheads since there's so much coke dealing going on.

I happen to be sitting next to the cop in the middle of

all these women, but of course for me it's all pure character research.

Travis looks out of his personal Winnebago and sees the women clustering around the cop and me, and for some reason he assumes it's me they're all fascinated by.

A couple of young Baptist lovelies are walking by his door on their way to join the enchanted throng and Travis gives them his big line:

'Hey girls! You wanna see my gun collection?'

(Travis is a gun nut and never travels without his personal collection of firearms.)

The young women give him a blank look and keep walking right on by to join the mesmerized throng around the handsome Hispanic cop.

Travis does not like being ignored and in his agitation speaks directly from the heart:

'Goddamn it! *I'm* the *star!*'

. . . and retreats into his lonely Winnebago.

After the car chases are finished it's time for the breasts.

Breasts are an essential part of every American independent film. Market forces being what they are, the only way to make money on an independent film is to sell it in Europe, and it is well-known that Europeans won't pay money for your film unless they are guaranteed to see some large American breasts. They like American violence too, but there's more control of cinematic violence than of cinematic sex in Europe.

Europeans have got some crackpot notion that exposure to violence is bad for you and that sex is somehow natural and not to be feared. In America we know that's exactly backward.

I once did a network TV series called *Dangerous Curves* about female private eyes with thigh holsters strapped up so high under their miniskirts that they ruptured themselves trying to quick draw. We shot two versions of each episode: one for the United States and one for Europe.

In one European episode we could show a man fondling a woman's naked breast. Of course something like that is totally banned on U.S. network television.

What we *could* show in the United States was a woman in a bra with a guy *cutting* her breast with a switchblade. No problem *there* with the American censors.

Anyway, the upcoming breast shot is a hot topic on set. The scene is poolside at Coy Harker's palatial redneck drug baron estate.

Coy is all stressed out because the Colombians are coming to kill him with chain saws. His girlfriend, played by Jane Badler, arranges a little soothing breast massage for him. Not Jane's breasts. Jane is a star, and her breasts don't come cheap. (She was in a mini series about aliens called *V,* and the second *Mission: Impossible* series.) Jane plays a kind of black widow in this movie. She sleeps with all the various drug lords and snuffs them as they lie in afterglow. But even though she has about four times as much sex as anybody in the movie, Jane never has to get nekkid. That's star power.

The owner of the commercially essential mammaries is Tiffany, an erotic dancer from one of the topless emporiums of the city. Tiffany is a knockout. Nature has blessed her with womanly attributes of a most spectacular quality.

A funny thing happens when you shoot a nude scene in a movie. All the crew start bustling around very professionally as if this were just another scene. The males especially get real dedicated. It's just a coincidence that they all seem to have essential duties to perform as close to the action as possible.

The women on the crew are gruff and business-like, but there's an undercurrent of tension because they know that the men are *enjoying* their work so much, all of a sudden.

The women also seem to be in conflict over the feeling of smug superiority they feel (*You'd never catch me flouncing around in front of these lowlifes!*) . . . and their natural reaction to a Code Red escalation in the war of biological competition (*Implants!*)

And then the poor Baptist intern girls are totally spazzed because by now they are sure that they're going to hell for working on the Devil's Soft-Porn/Action/Thriller.

The actors, on the other hand, are just trying to maintain. Nothing is worse than a nude love scene. If you think it's sexy facing a pair of twenty-twenty tits while forty people hang on your every reaction (or react to your every erection), then you should report to Masters and Johnson. (God knows what the naked woman feels like while eighty eyes peruse her. I suppose that if you're a topless dancer it's a bit of a yawn. Maybe Tiffany is the only relaxed person on the set.)

I am not involved in this carnal moment, to my great relief. Coy Harker has sent me off to perform the latest kidnapping on Renee O'Connor. I make my exit and then linger around the set, lending moral support to my fellow actors. Yeah, that's it.

The actor playing Coy is my buddy. He's one of the best actors in Texas and is doing a bang-up job playing a coked-up, stressed-out, chainsaw-fearing drug baron. But this scene has got him spooked. He confides in me that he has not yet been able to bring himself to inform his wife that he is soon to be on the receiving end of another woman's knockers. He and his wife are really in love, and it's kind of cute how this is bothering him.

OK, they're ready to roll. Coy is leaning back on a chaise lounge while Jane massages his shoulders. Jane calls across the pool to where Tiffany is oiling up.

'Tiffany! Could you help us out here?'

Tiffany undulates over to them and leans over Coy. She reaches around with one hand and unhooks her bikini top. Wham!

Say hallo to my not-so-leetle fraaands!

It gets very, very quiet on set.

Breasts are powerful things.

Just as Tiffany emerges, Coy shuts his eyes tight. He remains chastely blind through the rest of the scene as she rubs herself all over his hairy chest.

I guess Coy has adopted a strategy of plausible deniability. ('See honey? I didn't even look!')

This is the only scene in the movie that requires multiple takes.

It has now become impossible for anybody to ignore the fact that Travis absolutely hates me. It's just that all my stuff is going well and I'm coming up with these scene-stealing adlibs. And let's face it: Middle-aged oil men with lucky Colt .45s are a dime a dozen, but a true psycho-cowboy is a character to be savored.

My latest transgression is Dexter's death scene.

After about the third successful kidnapping of young

Renee, I leave her in the capable hands of big Dexter. Dexter has both Renee and Travis's girlfriend tied up in an icehouse. Travis finds them there and dispatches Dexter with an ice hook.

Dexter winds up frozen on an icy carpet of comic books.

I discover the body of my erstwhile friend and take full advantage of the moment by having a complete ad-libbed breakdown.

I cry piteously over my dead amigo. I beat poor Dexter on his massive frozen chest and cuss him out plaintively for getting killed and leaving me all alone. Then I boil over in rage and pursue Travis into the icehouse, spouting eloquent vows of vengeance. (Something like, 'I'll get you, you sonuvabitch!' Or maybe it was, 'Ready or not, here I come!')

Well, Director Frank loves my little moment, but when Travis sees my latest improv he is less than amused. He takes Frank into the backroom and pulls investor-rank on him. He demands that I not be allowed to cry. It develops too much sympathy for my character. (This after I have brutally kidnapped a teenager and been disrespectful to minorities, having shot several in the face.)

Travis wants to be the only one to cry. (Actually he had his chance in the first act and bonked it.)

Brave Frank, artistic integrity intact, resists this craven attempt to deny me my God-given right to emote. He banishes Travis to the Winnebago, and since several people have yet to be killed we proceed with the thinning of the cast.

In retrospect, I can only surmise what Travis's mental state must have been at this juncture, what weedy thoughts

were taking root in his loamy brain. Sitting there surrounded by his gun collection, hating me. Needing to
strike back at his tormentor. Needing somehow to win the
approval of Baptist girls everywhere.

I only know that something snapped.

The climactic moment of our film is when Coy Harker
gets the drop on Travis Winslow and makes him give up
his lucky Colt. Suddenly, I, Charlie Balace the psycho-
cowboy, arrive.

I have kidnapped yet another female victim, this time
Travis's girlfriend, played by Julia Montgomery. I carry
poor Julia in front of me like a shield and demand that my
partner Coy *give Travis his gun back*. This is because I
intend, with my demented cowboy sense of honor, to '*kill
him fair*'. Coy thinks I am Looney Tunes but complies
with my request.

Still ad-libbing, I place the barrel of my gun against
Julia's luxurious lips and hiss, with rage-provoking in-
souciance,

'*Kiss it for luck, honey!*'

I then cast her aside as Travis and I holster our guns and
stand across from each other in an old-fashioned Western
showdown.

I hate to spoil the suspense for you, but I'm about to get
dead.

Travis is supposed to beat me to the draw, naturally, and
then kill Coy and collapse into the arms of his loving
daughter and girlfriend. I mean, it's the standard ending
since Hoot Gibson.

The problem is, we are in independent film hell here.

We're down to the nubbin; we've been going all night and it's almost dawn. The crew has been exhausted, chemically augmented, and then exhausted again.

Likewise the budget.

And I only have one shirt.

This means we get only one chance to squib me and blow me away, because if we don't get it in one take, take two will have me standing there with a tattered bloody hole already adorning my thoroughly established ugly shirt.

Therefore, Frank is being extremely careful to explain the sequence and to double-check everything to make sure my death scene goes flawlessly.

Travis and I stand on our marks in the icehouse while the special effects guys flutter about and tell me exactly when to draw and where to land.

Protocol dictates that there is never to be a live round, blank or otherwise, in anybody's gun until the actual shot is to be fired. Basic safety rule. And horseplay with firearms is absolutely forbidden. Therefore Travis and I are standing there with empty guns. Ostensibly.

So before we do the fire in the hole shot, Frank wants to do close-ups of me and Travis giving each other steely, tension-enhancing, eyeball-to-eyeball-type showdown looks. I'm first, so they aim the camera at me and roll it.

What the hell, it's my death scene. Might as well throw in just one more ad-lib. I mean, why stop now?

I bare my teeth like Jack Palance and snarl:

'*Let's go, cowboy. Duel in the Sun!*'

Whereupon Travis draws his lucky Colt .45 and shoots my ass.

This comes as a shock. First of all, the sound of a .45 in a concrete icehouse is startling, to say the least. Second of all, nobody is expecting it. Especially not me.

Thinking I have somehow screwed up this pressure take, I react instinctively and fall backward on to the hard floor, writhing in my death agony.

Chaos.

Everybody rushes over to me. All the blood has drained out of Frank's face. He thinks Travis has actually shot me.

Travis is laughing contentedly. Evidently he has decided to teach me a lesson and secretly loaded his gun with his own blank ammo out in the Winnebago.

What a clever fellow.

What really scalds me is that we still haven't gotten the death scene and the bastard gets to shoot me again!

The movie comes out and looks great and everything. People at the festivals ooh and ahh over the car chases and Tiffany's breasts. The actor who plays Charlie Balace the psycho-cowboy receives glowing notices. (Especially my death scene, complete with properly exploded ugly shirt.)

About the only problem with *Black Snow* is the lead actor. People just don't respond to him.

How astonishing.

Frank winds up making a deal with a distributor who sells the movie in Europe and keeps all the money. Frank tells me that when he tries to get his contracted share, the distributor says, 'So sue me.'

The distributor evidently made deals for all the small films he could and then released them. Somehow that portion of the profits designated for the filmmakers was minimal to non-existant. Legal hijinx ensue, during which time the film remains unreleased in the United States.

Black Snow fell into a black hole.

As for me, Charlie Balace would have been a defining career moment . . . if the movie had ever been released.

Frank Patterson goes back to teaching. Ten years later he calls me up with another project. In fact he casts a lot of the main people from *Black Snow* (with a few notable exceptions) in his new movie, called *Roses*. It's a Romantic/Black Comedy/Woman's Picture.

We all go down to Florida and it's like old-home week.

Frank has severely curtailed my ability to improvise by having me play, in two-thirds of my scenes, a corpse. Nevertheless, *Roses* has been a big hit at the festivals.

But if Frank really wants to sell it, this time he'll put *me* on the poster instead of Tiffany.

Wishbone

I **HAVE A BIG FAN BASE** of five to-ten-year-olds. I get invited to speak at elementary schools and Cub Scout pack meetings. I'm a big draw at after-school library parties.

No, this is not because these kids have seen Chuck Norris beating me up on *Walker: Texas Ranger*.

Kids are in awe of me because *I* have worked with Wishbone.

If you are the parent of a preteen child, no explanation is necessary. You have no doubt watched *Wishbone* on your local PBS channel many, many times.

For the uninitiated, Wishbone is a dog. Not a big dumb slobber dog, but a genius Jack Russell terrier. He is the star of a series of the same name about adventures in suburbia with his master, young Joe Talbot, and neighborhood friends.

The purpose of this series (since it's on PBS it has to have a higher, educational purpose beyond mere entertainment) is to encourage elementary school kids to read books. So every week, Wishbone's contemporary adventures are paralleled in the plot of a literary classic. For instance, Joe Talbot might start an after-school job that gets out of hand and we'll see vignettes from the story of King Midas. These classical vignettes always star Wishbone as the lead character. So in that episode, for example, every time Wishbone tries to eat a dog biscuit it turns to gold.

Being the star also allows Wishbone to wear cute little doggie costumes with funny hats, rendering him irresistibly cuddly to the younger set. And while the kids are admiring Wishbone in a toga, they are presumably being subliminally implanted with a burning desire to read the Greek myths.

It's a worthwhile series with enormous appeal to kids. It's been a big success for PBS too. So why did it go to reruns after only a couple of dozen episodes?

First of all, PBS doesn't exactly shower you with cash when you make a series for them. And of course there are no commercials to sell.

Wishbone was relying on sales of little toy Wishbone dogs to finance the continuation of the series after the initial investment. Kids would be able to dress him up just like on TV.

Unfortunately, the company making the toy dogs completely bungled the job, coming in very late with the product and missing the Christmas season. When their prototype finally did show up it looked like a bad piñata. So there was no money for a second season.

After a year off, the producers came up with enough bread to make about six more episodes, but then had to fold the tents. By this time, the initially preteen actors who were playing Wishbone's human friends had grown breasts and mustaches and that adorable childhood ambience was somehow missing.

So that's why you parents have had to watch Wishbone

play King Midas about forty times. PBS just keeps rerunning the same episodes over and over.

This is a good deal for them, because PBS has a sweetheart contract that says they don't have to pay the actors anything for reruns. (I starred in a PBS series called *Newscast from the Past* that's been running for eighteen years: '*This is Marco of Padua reporting from Italy, where thousands are dying from the Black Death . . .*' (I made a grand total of one hundred dollars.) This is why I don't donate to public television during pledge drives; I figure I gave at the office.

I get to work in an episode called 'Rushin' to the Bone', where Wishbone gets cast as the spokesdog for a Mr. MacPooch dogfood commercial. This is somehow set up as a case of mistaken identity paralleling Nikolai Gogol's play *The Inspector General*.

I play the director of the commercial, Seymour LaVista. The actors performing the Russian interludes get to have the real fun, but I do get a golden opportunity to parody commercial directors.

I am allowed to have wardrobe input and come up with the quintessential auteur look: Banana Republic safari shirt with lots of pockets, designer jeans, and huge glasses with red frames equipped with a cord so I can dangle them from my neck. The final touch is a sweater carelessly shawled around my shoulders.

The actual director of our episode kind of winces when he meets me on the set. I've hit close to home.

My first scene is the audition where Joe Talbot brings Wishbone in for his reading. It's delightful to sit behind the desk for a change and come on like King Herod.

Wishbone himself isn't present while we shoot my
dialogue. I have to talk to the piñata, sitting obediently
at Joe's feet. No matter. I'm having a blast waving my arms
around in self-important passion, demanding the dog to
act 'perky'.

This is an inside joke that only someone who has gone
through a commercial audition can appreciate. The ad-
vertising industry is always looking for smiling happy faces
to rhapsodize about the life-saving attributes of various
toothpastes and floor cleaners. (I must plead guilty to
actually saying the words '*I'm in love with my burger!*' in a
restaurant commercial.) In the commercial world, the
code word for such saccharine behavior is 'perky'.

After I have finished my antics, the star comes out to
shoot the reverse angle.

At this point, make sure all your children have left the
room. If any tender psyches are to be traumatized, let it be
on *your* head.

I'm about to spill the beans: There are actually *two*
Wishbones.

There's a Close-up Wishbone and a Stunt Wishbone.
All the shots of Wishbone running through the woods
leaping over fallen logs are played by Stunt Wishbone. All
the cute and cuddly shots of Wishbone doing back flips
and chasing his tail and adorably cocking his head to the
side are portrayed by Close-up Wishbone.

I bet they wish they could do this with Tom Cruise.

Anyhow, they bring Close-up Wishbone out to do his
thing. They shoot about four tricks and reward the dog
with Kibbles & Bits. Takes about five minutes and he's
gone. His stuff will be edited into footage of Joe Talbot
looking proud and me waving my arms around.

I almost make a big mistake. I start to pet the dog. The crew hisses at me just in time. The one immutable law on the set of *Wishbone* is Don't Touch the Dog. They have a large woman with a cattle prod stationed nearby in case you forget.

This is necessary because with a hundred people on the set, the cute little Jack Russell would soon be stroked bald if they didn't have this rule.

Actually I ran into a similar situation on a Drew Barrymore movie.

After Wishbone aces the audition we get to do the big scene on the soundstage where we shoot the Mr. Mac-Pooch commercial. We've got twenty dancers in kilts waving flags around. They roll out a tartan carpet for Wishbone, who is supposed to make a grand entrance in his little doggie kilt.

The plot calls for Wishbone to freeze up because he's embarrassed to be wearing a 'dress'. This sends my Seymour LaVista character into some kind of grand mal seizure of artistic frustration. And since they have given me a megaphone, my feelings become emphatically known.

The director calls me aside.

'Could you tone it down a little bit? This is a family show.'

'But my character is very angry.'

'I know. But I need a *family* kind of anger.'

'You mean, internalize my anger more?'

'I mean, try not to make the children's teeth bleed.'

'Gotcha.'

They bring Close-up Wishbone over for a dialogue

shot with me. They shoot Wishbone from behind my legs and down low. This gives the illusion that the dog is looking at me. What he's really looking at is the kibble in his trainer's extended hand. The trainer is crouching just behind me. The kibble goes left . . . Wishbone tilts his head left. The kibble goes right . . . Yeah, you got it.

They let the guy who provides the voice of Wishbone do Wishbone's lines from an offstage mike. This allows us humans to time *our* lines right, so they can edit more easily.

The voice guy is a witty fellow who likes to entertain with little quips. Since I am the villain of the piece, most of these quips are at my expense.

I hate ad-libbers when they're not me.

Joe Talbot and his friends and family become aware that Wishbone is not happy playing Mr. MacPooch. So they stand up to my tirades and walk off the set, taking their dog friend back home where he's happy.

The moral of our story sets up very nicely with the PBS agenda. I guess it would be something subtle like: '*Crass commercialism is bad for small furry creatures.*' Or maybe: '*Commercial television will corrupt your children and make your dog's soul rot in hell.*'

In reality, if you walked off the set of a national TV commercial, corporate lawyers would descend like banshees and legally suck the very marrow from your wishbones.

I have a stock routine when I speak at the children's functions to which I am invited because of my fame as a *Wishbone* alumnus. You see, the kids always ask the same question: 'How do they get Wishbone to wear all those costumes?'

I tell them, 'It's easy. They just reach down behind his ear and turn off the switch. Then he's nice and still while they dress him.'

(Blank looks.)

'Oh! You mean to tell me you thought he was a *real dog!* That's a *robot!* They could never get a *real* dog to do that stuff!'

Oh the Shock. The Outrage. The Mortification.

And that's just from the mommies.

Walk Away, Renée

IT STINKS IN THIS CHICKEN COOP.

But I don't complain. That's because while I am *sitting* in chicken shit, the director is across from me actually *lying* in chicken shit.

Bob Markowitz has stationed himself in the only vacant corner of this edifice so he can watch me act. He could have just sent in his camera operator to get the shot and watched it all on video in the relative comfort of the barnyard. But that's not the kind of guy he is. Bob is that rarest of birds . . . the Sensitive Director. He's a hands-on guy who insists on getting down in the trenches with the troops.

He's lying on his belly with his head peeking out from under the camera, trying to get a low-angle shot of me having a Real Moment.

And it just doesn't get any Realer than chicken shit.

There's very little room in a chicken coop for sizable mammals like humans. Three of us . . . Bob, the camera operator, and me . . . pretty much fill up the available space. There's not even any room for the key components of the scene:

Bodies. Dead bodies.

There's supposed to be three dead people in here with us. But there's no room to put them.

We're shooting a TV movie called *Murder in the Heartland*. It's about Charlie Starkweather and his fourteen-year-old girlfriend, Caril, who went on a wild killing spree in Nebraska back in the fifties. The first people they killed were Caril's parents and baby sister. Charlie shot them and hid them in the chicken coop.

I play Bob, Caril's brother-in-law and ex–best friend of Charlie. I have come over to my in-laws' farm and discovered the evidence of the crime.

My problem as an actor is that, because we have no room for the bodies, there is no *evidence* for me to see and react to. This is not exactly a comedy scene, and I don't want to fake it. Squinting like Clint won't work. The bad-laxative commercial tear squeeze is to be avoided at all costs. I must honor the dead with a Real Moment.

Bob Markowitz waits patiently in his bed of manure for me to prepare.

I notice a broken doll in a pile of trash in a dark corner of the coop. I get an idea. I grab the doll and place it where the bodies are supposed to be. I focus on that pathetic little broken doll for a minute and then tell Bob that I'm ready.

'ROLL IT . . . ACTION!'

And it happens. I start sobbing from deep in my guts. After a few seconds I slowly turn away and stagger out the door of the coop into the barnyard, where cast and crew wait shivering in the damp Texas morning. I'm still sobbing long after the scene cuts.

Bob comes out and pats me on the back. 'Great job.'

Tim Roth comes over and says something complimentary. Tim is playing Starkweather. He's so good in this role that you kind of tense up when he's near you. He's scary good.

Renée Zellweger brings me a drink of water. Renée is playing my wife (and Caril's sister), Barbara. She kids me: 'That was some damn fine blubbering! Better than yesterday, huh?'

Now I'm laughing. That's the weird thing about acting. One minute you're lost in some quasi-real moment where your emotions are churning. Then you snap back to actual life. Then you have to go mood up for the next slice of quasi-life,

Renée is referring to our scene yesterday, when things got fairly ludicrous.

Now, even though Renée is an unknown at this point in her career, the girl has obviously got it. She's one of those rare people who just seems to be more *alive* than everybody else. That quality translates emphatically onto film. But at twenty-some years of age there are a few life experiences that have as yet remained outside her sphere. One of them is motherhood.

The scene in question has Renée and me driving up to the house in a cab. We've come to show off our new baby to Renée/Barbara's mom. We don't know that her mom is stashed out in the chicken coop already and that Charlie Starkweather is waiting inside the house with his shotgun to kill us if we come inside.

Sister Caril, played by Fairuza Balk, comes out to scare us away and save our lives.

The scene calls for Renée to hop out of the car with the baby and walk up to the house while I wait in the cab. Her sister comes out and yells at Renée that everybody has the flu and she has to go away or the baby will catch it.

As they often do on films, they've hired a set of twins to

take turns being our baby. That way if one twin doesn't cooperate they can substitute the other one and stay on schedule.

So Renée and I are sitting in the backseat of the cab ready to start the scene. They hand Renée the first girl baby.

The baby takes one look at Renée and starts yelling.

They can't start the scene until the baby is quiet or the sound track will be saturated with crying and the rest of the dialogue won't be heard.

Renée does her best. She bounces the baby on her knee and makes goo-goo noises. The baby is not buying it. It's not Renée's fault. She just hasn't had much practice at this sort of thing.

I tell her to give the kid to me for a minute.

Being a good deal older than Renée I have plumbed some of the depths of these mysteries. I use a tried-and-true method. I put the squalling infant against me and start humming 'Old Man River' deep down in my chest, where it vibrates against her cheek. In about thirty seconds the little girl is mesmerized. Works every time.

I carefully hand her back to Renée, while signaling to the crew that we're ready to roll. As soon as Renée puts her hands on the baby the spell is broken. Her little eyes pop open and she lets out a yowl.

I take the little howler back and give her another dose of basso profundo susurration. In five seconds she is staring up at me in quiet fascination.

I glance at Renée. If looks could kill.

I shrug apologetically. 'They like old musicals.'

We try it again. Ever so delicately we try to transfer the hypnotized child from my arms to Renée's.

'WAAAAAANHH!'

Instant eruption.

The crew groans and Bob Markowitz comes over to the car. 'What's the matter?'

'This baby hates me,' Renée replies.

'Not to worry, we've got other babies,' Bob reassures her. 'Bring in the Back-up Baby!'

So they bring in the second twin and hand this one to Renée. And what happens next?

To save time just reread the previous two pages.

They wind up reworking the scene so the baby stays quietly in the car with me, while Renée gets out and does her dialogue. Renée brings a certain icy fury to the material that is quite effective, I think.

If you listen really closely you can hear ' . . . *He don't plant taters . . . He don't plant cotton . . .*' coming from the cab in the background.

I have recovered from my chicken coop meltdown. All the emotional fuel necessary for twenty seconds of acting has been consumed and I am hollow. Such a peculiar way to make a living, I think, as Renée and I walk back to the honey wagon. It's a cold, overcast, winter day in McKinney, Texas.

By coincidence, my grandfather was raised in McKinney, on a farm much like this. My feelings are awash in a combination of post–chicken coop quasi-trauma and family nostalgia. I need a break. We have several hours of downtime before we are required to gas up for another Magic Moment.

Renée is in a chirpy mood. Despite her effect on babies she is doing quite well in her small part. She is feeling heartened. Like me, Renée is an Austin actor. She is one of a clutch of apprentice starlets who drop in on my acting class now and then to 'hone their instrument'.

Having had small parts in a few films seems to have qualified me as an eminence grise in the Austin film community. I teach a weekly film-acting workshop. Renée and her friends often ask my advice on this or that aspect of the business.

Renée asks for feedback. I tell her she doesn't need my advice. She's doing just great. Of course she doesn't believe me, and continues to pester me for pearls of wisdom. I tell her she's got some major wattage going for her. There's the camera. Sic 'em!

Now she's happy.

We agree that it's bound to be a long time before they need us. We joke that we hope it's a *really* long time and we rack up some overtime pay. Heaven is lying in your trailer sawing Z's while you're getting paid time-and-a-half.

Still recovering from my actor's epiphany, I am ready for a snooze. Renée won't let me. She's wired and wants to hang out. We decide to play cards.

She comes into my trailer dressing room and plops down on the couch. 'It's freezing in here. Let's close the door and turn on the heater.'

Uh . . . how do I put this. A movie set is kind of like a Dante's *Inferno* of gossip. A closed door is asking for it. I can just see the news being passed around the set from walkie-talkie to walkie-talkie: 'Marco and three Teamsters just went into a room with Renée Zellweger . . . details to follow!'

I gingerly explain this to Renée; sweet, young, innocent thing that she is. I'm trying to be delicate, and at first she doesn't understand what the fuss is all about. 'You mean we have to sit here freezing to death?'

Well, actually . . . yes. I think it would be preferable. People could get the Wrong Idea.

'Oh brother! What a world! Here. I'll fix it.'

Renée stands up and goes over to the open door of my dressing room and yells out an announcement:

'ATTENTION EVERYBODY!'

A few curious grips look up. The Teamster truck drivers peer over their newspapers. An assistant holds up her walkie-talkie in readiness.

'I JUST WANT EVERYBODY TO KNOW THAT I'M CLOSING THIS DOOR SO WE CAN GET WARM, AND THIS DOESN'T MEAN WE'RE HAVING SEX! WE'RE PLAYING CARDS! WE'RE NOT SCREWING! NO HANKY-PANKY HERE! EVERYBODY RELAX! NO SEX! NO SEX! NO SEX!'

She slams the door and comes back to the couch.

'Deal.'

My reputation is saved.

Good-Time Charlie

I **T TOOK GOVERNMENT** intervention to get this movie made.

I'm working on a flick called *The Chase*, with Charlie Sheen and Kristy (*Buffy the Vampire Slayer*) Swanson. This film asks the hypothetical question: What if a criminal on the run (even though he's an innocent man) were to kidnap a girl (whose daddy turns out to be the richest man in California)? And then light out for the border in her BMW?

The answer, as it's been in all three hundred other desperate-criminal-kidnaps-the-girl movies made since 1930, is written in stone: They'll be heavily into the nookie by the middle of the second act.

Does that BMW have to have bucket seats?

The kidnapping takes place in a convenience store. That's where the government intervention comes in.

The producers are shooting this feature in Texas, but the story is supposed to be taking place in California. So they need to find places in Texas with palm trees and boats.

The locations people come up with this one 7-Eleven south of Houston that's near a marina. Trouble is, the manager of the 7-Eleven doesn't want to close his store for three days. He tells the Hollywood boys to take a hike.

This jeopardizes the whole shoot, which might have to relocate to Florida. A hundred local jobs hang in the balance.

Somebody calls Governor Ann Richards, who gets on the phone to national 7-Eleven headquarters and brokers a deal. The essential convenience store is ours.

I think they offer Ann a part in the movie. 'The woman rides a Harley; let's make her a highway patrolman.'

I'm playing a cop for the umpteenth time. It didn't start out this way. No, I was tapped for bigger things.

A supporting role, dripping with juicy dialogue. Pregnant with comic potential. Stinking with the musky scent of stolen scenes.

But the cup was dashed from my lips ere I had begun to quaff it.

I know just who to blame too. It's all the fault of Nicolas Cage.

Barbara Brinkley is the casting director. She got me cast as Clancy Pogue and has been calling me in for anything that requires tobacco chewing ever since.

Well, there's this real important role in *The Chase* that nobody thinks they can cast in Texas: a lawyer with Tourette's syndrome.

Now, you have to admit, political correctness aside, that's a pretty good comic premise:

'*Ladies and gentlemen of the jury . . .*
Whooooop-whooop! Shit! Fuck! Whoop! Whoop!'

It's a fun thing to audition for, and Barbara has sold them on at least looking at me.

I decide to be very earnest and sincere. Even when the guy is whooping, he has his client's best interests at heart. So I go in there and play it real serious while I'm twitching and strangling on cuss words, and the Hollywood boys collapse in a heap on the floor.

I am stardust. I am golden.

So I'm clearing my schedule for a nice three-week engagement when Barbara calls me.

The producer's brother is a friend of Nicolas Cage. He describes the role of the Tourette's lawyer to Nick and how funny it is. Next thing you know, Nicolas has cleared *his* schedule so *he* can do the damn part.

In between his multimillion dollar blockbusters.

I have been erased.

Out of pity they throw me a bone. That's how I get to be the cop.

Appropriately, most of *The Chase* takes place on the freeway as Charlie and Kristy race for the border with a fleet of police cars on their tail. The schedule calls for about twenty shooting days out on various highways around Houston.

So naturally they schedule the thing for July.

Alex and I are just as glad to be shooting our scenes in the 7-Eleven. At least it's air-conditioned, and air-conditioning is life itself in Houston in July.

Alex Morris is playing the other cop. He's a big African American dude who can really act. I mean, he does Shakespeare at the Alley Theatre. Just the kind of acting preparation you need to say lines like 'Can I see your license, please?'

Plotwise, Alex and I drive up to the 7–Eleven and notice Charlie Sheen's car outside, a car that Charlie's character did not legally purchase. So we go inside and Charlie freaks and grabs Kristy Swanson and shoves a Butterfinger candy bar in her back like it's a pistol. He makes us lie on the floor and takes our guns. Then he shoves Kristy into her BMW, and *The Chase* is on. (He lets Kristy eat the candy bar.)

Doesn't seem like much, but that little snippet will take sixteen hours to film.

Kristy Swanson is pouting. She has just found out that Charlie Sheen has a *penthouse* at the best hotel in town while she only has a *suite* at the best hotel in town. That could be a deal breaker. Many frantic calls to her L.A. agents. Pressure is brought to bear, and the producers quickly cave. Kristy gets a penthouse.

It's tough being a star. You've got to defend your turf. If word got around that you could get away with giving Kristy Swanson a suite instead of a penthouse, nobody would take her seriously as an actress any more.

These are the kinds of battles that are fought on a movie set.

Meanwhile, Alex and I are praying for overtime so we can qualify for health insurance.

Not that I begrudge Kristy Swanson anything.

In addition to being talented, Kristy Swanson is a peach. Kristy Swanson is the dope. Kristy Swanson is a healthy female of marriageable age.

Kristy Swanson is so beautiful that millions of people will go to see this movie just to look at her in a miniskirt. Many more millions will watch *The Chase* on television, and more millions will rent the video and keep rewinding to the part where she straddles Charlie Sheen on the bucket seat of the BMW and booglerizes him at ninety miles per hour.

And these millions of people will spend millions of dollars to look upon the wonder of Kristy's pulchritude and the use she makes of it. And part of those millions will trickle down to me, in the form of residuals, for years to come.

And lo, I will qualify for health insurance therefrom.

And so I say to Kristy, 'May the good Lord bless you and provide you with penthouses.'

I am grateful to Charlie Sheen too.

Charlie gets a bad rap. People think he's a lightweight actor and a party boy.

Well . . . he *is* a party boy. Or, at least, was.

But he's not a lightweight actor.

Everybody thinks that the really *good* actors are those English guys like Daniel Day Lewis and Ralph Fiennes. I agree. They're great.

But you never see them doing what Charlie Sheen does. Namely, screwball comedy.

Doing some gut-wrenching death scene that wrings emotion out of every pore is challenging. But it's elementary compared to sticking a Butterfinger in Kristy Swanson's back and pretending it's a gun and looking toward the camera with *just . . . the right . . . expression* to make the audience laugh.

That's a talent not everybody has. Like somebody once said: 'Dying is easy; comedy is hard.'

As far as the party boy thing, that's because of his handicap.

Charlie's handicap is that he's so rich and handsome and famous that women take off their panties when he clears his throat.

For Alex and me, the main problem in this scene is finding a comfortable spot to sit that's out of camera range.

We're stuck in the 7-Eleven. They don't want us going back to the honey wagon over by the marina because every once in a while they need us in the background for some panoramic shot of Kristy cruising the aisles for Ding Dongs.

It'll be hours before we shoot any of our dialogue. They try to make us go outside and hang around, but we whine real good about how hot our cop uniforms are and how we'll get all sweaty and have to go back to makeup. So they let us camp out over by the comic books.

Alex's teenage son comes to visit his dad on the set and he camps out with us. This helps pass the time because now we have someone to tease.

Many hours go by while Kristy and Charlie go up and down the aisles of the store with the camera crew scuttling behind them.

The film industry has just discovered that shaky, hand-held look. It's so cutting edge that every movie, TV show and commercial being made this year is using it simultaneously, therefore rendering it instantly overdone and obnoxious.

I hate first days. The director is always trying to make his mark by showing off his coverage chops.

They've finally shot Kristy searching for Ding Dongs from every possible angle: wide, medium, closeup, steadicam and shaky-cam.

Now they have to repeat the whole rigmarole with Charlie.

It's almost dinnertime, and all Alex and I have done is read every comic book on the 7-Eleven rack.

Our 'big scene' doesn't make great demands upon the instrument. We're supposed to stand there with our hands up and then lie down on the floor. My big line is something like, *'Take it easy, buddy! All you got so far is a stolen car rap!'*

All the inactivity has overprimed my pump. I'm trying to make too much out of my 'moment'.

This is how Bad Acting happens.

I think I'm still subconsciously resentful that the Tourette's lawyer part has been ripped from my sweaty grasp. I'll show them!

I start living the moment to the hilt. I'm just so *angry!* I'm so *intense!* I'm so . . . *sucky!*

I'm grinding my teeth and twitching my nose. My eyes are rolling around and I'm flicking my tongue at Charlie.

If Mark Fuhrman had Tourette's syndrome, this is what he'd look like.

'T-T-T-Take it eeeezzy, b-buddy! (shlobber-gnash-foam). Allssh you gotchsofar (spit-foam) is a s-s-s-stolen car rap! (snarl-foam-whoop!)'

I think the director is relieved when he can finally make me lie down on the floor.

So there we are: the kid playing the store clerk, Alex and me — all facedown on the nasty floor with our hands outstretched. Charlie's got his arm around Kristy's waist as he shoves the candy bar in her back. This tends to hike up Kristy's already severely curtailed mini-garment.

Observant actors that we are, we floor-huggers register this fact and gallantly avert our eyes.

'No! No! No! Keep looking at them! Keep looking at them!'

Not being down here on the floor with our point of view, our director is missing the significance of our self-sacrificing gesture.

Oh well. Orders is orders.

We all dutifully focus on the stars. Ms. Swanson's tanned legs fill our horizon.

On action, Kristy starts squirming. She's probably not aware of the effect of this on her floor-bound costars. Either that or she is making a noble gesture of her own.

Alex and I exchange a look. We're making a supreme effort to stay in distressed, sullen cop mode.

Lord! *Hep* me now!

Several takes later the director asks us if we need a break.

'Nah. It's OK. Might as well stay down here. How about you, Alex?'

'Nah. I'm fine. Wouldn't want to lose my mark.'

'Shoot as many takes as you need. We're perfectly all right. Really.'

It's evening now, and word has spread around the sub-urban Houston neighborhood that there's somebody famous down at the marina. People are showing up and surrounding the convenience store, waiting to get a glimpse of a movie star. The security guys have to string up a rope two hundred feet back from the set to keep the bedazzled herd from stampeding right into the store.

You'd think we were giving away free beer.

Our movie stars are hip to this development and stay inside between takes. I strike up a conversation with Charlie.

Actually, I pass on a compliment. Charlie starred in a movie called *Navy SEALS* a few years ago. My stepson is a Navy SEAL, and he happened to tell me that the film's depictions of SEAL training and procedure were surprisingly accurate. I say surprisingly because Hollywood routinely botches details like this. (See *G.I. Jane.*)

When I tell Charlie that his film gets the official SEAL seal of approval, his face lights up. He starts telling me how hard they worked trying to get it right and how gratifying it is to get the compliment.

I believe the guy really gives a damn.

Alex and I are finally wrapped at one o'clock in the morning. We've been inside that fluorescent box for so long that the steamy Houston night is downright refreshing.

Out beyond the ropes, at the shadowy edge of the work light periphery, we sense a stirring. A buzz starts up, like the thrumming of bees.

What gives?

Oh my God. It's the fans.

At one A.M. on a weekday night, they're still out there . . . waiting. Hundreds of people standing behind the ropes.

The thrumming subsides. The fans have registered that Alex and I are mere roughage.

They want meat.

I go back inside and tell Charlie that his public awaits.

Charlie is used to this. He and Kristy are waiting for the limo to drive up to the door of the 7-Eleven.

Charlie is feeling frisky. A long day in the confines of the convenience store has given him a taste for other climes. He asks me if I care to accompany him into the city to see what pleasures the night might bring.

A little late for me, thanks. Maybe some other time. And then my wife can let me have it with the meat axe.

The stretch limo pulls up to the store. There's a coital moan from the fans. I shake hands goodbye with everybody and slip outside to witness this Hollywood moment.

The folks outside the ropes are on tiptoe, tangibly parturient with anticipation. Some are holding up their sleepy kids and telling them to get ready for the great moment when those *very special people* will walk out the door and validate them.

What is this strange force that compels these people to wait out here in the dark all night *just to look at Charlie Sheen?* What kind of hideous hunger of the spirit is nourished by such a meager helping of celebrity?

Kristy and Charlie step out of the store into a clapping, cheering, Sea of Love.

The movie stars pull back those ravishing lips and expose those perfect teeth in incandescent acceptance of this adoration.

They turn to the left and wave. They turn to the right and wave. Regnant with glamour.

Worship them! Worship them!

One more smile. One more wave.

And into the limo they climb.

The luxury automobile speeds off into the darkness, bearing its precious cargo of young gods back to Olympian penthouses in the sky.

The fans watch them go. Their moment of electric proximity to fame already just a happy memory.

They pick up their tired children and their dead six-packs and Grandma's lawn chair and melt away into the mundanity of their suburban tract homes.

Satiated by this strange exchange of energies. Stronger somehow. Redeemed.

Oh hell! I have to go back. I forgot to get my snapshot. The one of Kristy and Charlie with me standing between them.

I need it for my scrapbook.

Top Dog in the Big Apple

KNOW I CAN'T TELL YOU anything about New York that you don't already know. Even if I did you wouldn't admit it. No one can afford to admit that he or she is not up on life in the Apple. To do so would be to admit terminal unhipness. Or, perhaps, dis-hippity. After all, if you 'can make it there you can make it anywhere,' so the corollary renders you suspect.

This being said, I will tell you about my trip to New York, knowing all the while that I am not telling you anything new.

When you write about New York you have to get real gritty. New Yorkers like grit. This is one of the things they're most proud of. The fact that they are used to grit and can handle it and you'd better be able to handle it too if you wanna come to *my* town goddamn it.

People who read about New Yorkers expect a lot of grit in their prose, so I've been practicing. How about this:

'Her face was like the pavement: cold, hard and gritty.'

Or:

'He had a laugh like a power sander with grit in the bearings.'

This is one of my favorites:

'The snarling cop nightsticked me to my knees and left me searching for my teeth in the gritty snow.'

OK. I think I'm ready.

Jay is my video/film producer friend in Houston. He calls me up to hire me for a job hawking new Top Dog diesel fuel additive. It keeps your gas from 'gelling' up in the cold. We have to shoot it in the snow. No snow in Houston, ergo . . . road trip!

The western USA being dry as a bone thus far in the winter of '96, Jay books passage to NYC where they have an abundance of white stuff. And since you can't find actors in New York, Jay decides to bring me along. I guess he justifies this to the client somehow. I am billed as the definitive young trucker.

Off we fly to Newark. Doug the soundman joins us. I don't know why Jay has to bring his own soundman since he's hiring the rest of the crew in New York. I guess Doug has something on him. We all schlep equipment over to the rental van and head into the burg.

Jay used to live in New York and drive cabs and delivery vans and such stuff that aspiring young directors have to do while they aspire. So of course the minute we cross the bridge into Manhattan he switches into New York cabby mode.

This involves constant acceleration and no downshifting.

A New York cabby downshifts for nobody. A lot of lane changing occurs on all the one-way streets too. All the while Jay keeps up a running commentary on how New York cabbies are the best drivers in the world and the street system is so intelligently organized and you have to be looking thirty car lengths ahead at all times. All of this punctuated with outbursts of profanity at anybody who slows down to turn left or doesn't slow down to let Jay change lanes. These people, Jay informs us, are assholes. They must be chastised.

'Out of the way, asshole! Watch out, asshole! Let me in, asshole! That's right! Slow down, why don't you? Asshole!'

Of course all these people are calling Jay an asshole at the same time. We are all assholes together, careening around the borough. One big dysfunctional traffic family.

Doug and I have no assholes any more. They have closed up very tight indeed with Jay driving.

Our first stop is Katz's Delicatessen, where they filmed Meg Ryan having a simulated orgasm in that *When Harry Met Sally* movie. They have signs and pictures of this event put up on the walls.

I was in a movie with Meg a few years ago called *DOA*. I played a cab driver and Meg was in the backseat handcuffed to Dennis Quaid. There were no discernible orgasms that I was aware of.

I eat a sacramental pastrami sandwich that should satisfy all my animal fat requirements for the next quarter century. Jay likes delis. He tells us about all these fabulous delis he's going to take us to. The main criteria for judging a deli, according to Jay, is the quality of something called a 'knish'. Another factor is the creativity of insulting behavior by the proprietors.

'Tomorrow morning I'll take you to this little Ukrainian deli over on Second Avenue. The knishes are great and these Ukrainians are really rude!'

First we must find our hotel. Jay has offered Doug and I a choice between a sumptuous Hilton just across the river in New Jersey and a more humble (if also more convenient) Midtown affair. Doug and I both prefer to be in the very heart of the beast and so we are delivered. Grittiness awaits.

I am escorted to a room of some twenty square feet with a bed and a safe. The safe is actually a little larger than the bed. Definitely more comfortable. There is a closet of sorts consisting of a bar hanging over the bed so that your overcoat hangs down over your face. There is a gap of four inches all around the air-conditioning unit in the window. A well-ventilated room at least. I launch into my actor prima donna routine until Jay purchases an 'upgrade', which entitles me to a slightly larger room with a bigger safe.

We spend the afternoon in Times Square buying half-price theater tickets and drinking. Then we dress for our first big evening in the city. I choose a power blazer combo with a confident red tie and my official Bogart overcoat.

Jay tells me I am way overdressed for off-Broadway and will be sneered at by those in the know. He says I am an artist and artists don't have to wear ties. I think he's just jealous because he didn't bring one and feels hopelessly outclassed by my obvious sartorial splendor. Anyway I am taking no chances. Without the proper armoring I could be mistaken for a tourist, and that would be it. Subterranean crocodiles would drag me down as I scurry across the steaming subway grates. The gritty grates.

As all of you New York experts know, it is imperative to hurry when you are moving through the city. Even the slightest pause to study some architectural feature, store window, or woman's anatomy can instantly mark you as someone who has no driving, hectic New York Purpose and may therefore be cut down with impunity. It is also very helpful to have an impressive overcoat. I am so glad I didn't wear my dorky parka even though it is ten degrees.

The most essential item in my protective coloring is a carefully structured look of fierce contempt, which I turn upon all who cross my path as I stride purposefully toward the subway entrance. And of course you know the eye contact rule. As in none *ever* if you know what's good for you.

Funny thing though. As I course the stoic sidewalks of the hallowed burg, just about everybody I pass makes eye contact with me. I am powerless to prevent myself from responding in kind. Even though my busier-than-thou look of sneering truculence is carefully in place, I realize that just about everybody sneaks a little look at my eyeballs and I at theirs. I decide that this is a basic jungle law of the trail. Just a quick check of the windows of the soul to answer the important question: 'Is this guy a psycho killer?' Or in some cases: 'Are you impressed with my overcoat?' There's a hopeful and plaintive human quality here in the heart of the heartless city. One woman actually *speaks* to me as we pass like dories in the dusk. 'Lovely day, isn't it?' I jump off the sidewalk and hide under a parked taxicab. When she is safely gone I find a policeman and have her arrested as a dangerous lunatic.

But this is a trend. Steeled as I am for my urban interface, I am delightfully surprised at the good humor, helpfulness and, yes, politeness of the New Yorkers with whom my path converges on this little expedition.

The theater mavens at the off-Broadway house salute me in camaraderie. The Japanese waiters at the sushi bar where Jay and Doug go afterward (leaving me to wander the windy streets outside, where I am safe from raw octopi), greet me like a long-lost brother. The pink-haired young man lined up on the sidewalk for some mysterious rave is pleasantly civil. He answers my query as to the nature of the proceedings: 'I have no fucking idea, man. Got any smokes?'

Even the threatened contumacy of the Ukrainian deli owner whom we visit the next morning is blunted by affability. He gives me a free knish.

What has happened to New York? Where is Lou Reed? Has the blizzard of '96 so crushed with snow the fragile infrastructure that people tread quietly, afraid that any violent outburst may cause an avalanche? Maybe it's that I'm from Texas. So hopelessly provincial that city dwellers can afford to let their guard down a little and enjoy the entertainment possibilities inherent in my behavior.

Jay has cleverly arranged our punishing schedule so that we have a whole day free to 'scout locations'. I decide to scout the art museums. My only other assignment is to procure some hair dye.

Jay, after knowing me for fifteen years, has suddenly discovered that my hair is graying. 'Goddamn it! Why is your hair gray? You're supposed to be the *young* trucker! Hell, you look older than the guy I got to play the *old* trucker!'

Jay thinks all this criticism disconcerts me, but unlike

other fatuous actors I am much too handsome to be vain. I agree to buy a tankard of chocolate thunder if it will shut him up.

My guides to the cultural nexii are Mimi and Arthur. Mimi and I lived together for a brief time in the 1970s and in a real tribute to therapy have somehow remained friends. Or more likely the brain cells responsible for retaining memories of that era are so hopelessly fried that we have no actual recollection of each other at all.

Arthur is another refugee from that decade of excess who spent most of it driving a Land Rover across Africa, Asia Minor and the Indian subcontinent. He can tell a couple of stories. He seems to be most proud of the fact that after his travels he sold the Land Rover for the same price he paid for it. He now writes a financial column. They have a five-year-old named Ian and live in a house in Greenwich Village with a backyard. This is pretty hot shit in New York, but Texans just laugh.

We go to the Museum of Modern Art and look at Monet's water lilies and all those other fabulous paintings by those fabulous art dudes. Then we go hair dye hunting.

When I describe to Arthur the nature of my quest he chuckles indulgently and assures me that this being New York, I can find it. But each all-night drug emporium I enter has the same rack of semipermanent hair schlock. The Clairol jobbers have been bending some knees around here and forcing out the Roux Fanci-full products I use for all my hair coloring needs. You see, my brand of happy juice washes out with my next shampoo, unlike the alternatives, which fade over a period of three weeks to a vivid orange.

We hit most of the downtown spots with no luck.

Finally I find a half-full bottle of Espresso Delight in the back of a Puerto Rican five-and-dime. I negotiate with the proprietor for a discount and carefully store my prize in the pocket of my overcoat.

Arthur has gotten all excited about Indian food after regaling me with tales of the Hindu Kush, and we eat curry at a place he remembers from his bachelorhood. Alas, times have changed. We wind up poisoning ourselves with stale tandoori bread and old chutney. We decide to go to the movies to cheer up.

When we get home I realize that my precious, hard-won happy juice has slipped out of my overcoat pocket at the movie, and I am back to square one, hair dye-wise.

Today is our first actual day of media labor, and off we go to the wilds of Jersey and the famed Crossroads Diner, our main location for principal photography.

Upon arrival Jay immediately establishes dominance over his all-union New York crew by barking at them about camera angles and fills while I slip down to the local shopping center to renew my quest for youth in a bottle. I am gratified to learn that the Clairol Mafia has not sabotaged competitive capitalism in the state of New Jersey. I return to the diner a stunning brunette.

In my absence . . . disaster. The mock-up cans of Top Dog diesel fuel additive, recently Fed Exed from Houston, have been lost by our client's hotel. Any other calamity can be overcome. If the camera breaks, we can get another. If an actor breaks, likewise. If the director has an attack of mad cow disease and starts foaming at the mouth he can be sedated and quietly driven to Bellevue and the show can go on. But when you're making a commercial, the actor has to hold up a can of the product and say, 'This stuff saved my very soul!' And we have no product. Everybody goes home until replacements can be found.

I use this unplanned paid vacation day to continue my cultural tour of the city. I get the New York crew to drive me in. They take me by way of the Meadowlands and try to scare me with tales of Jimmy Hoffa buried in the swamps of Jersey. (Like all union guys they are proud of their traditions.) They make me swear not to take a cab while I am touring the city. Real men take the subway. At least real men who don't own a grip truck.

I bid them farewell until tomorrow and dash in to the Planetarium, where I am just in time for the last afternoon show. I pay my eight dollars and sit back in the seat. They turn out the lights and I immediately go to sleep. An eight-dollar nap is what I have. After the show I choke back to life and stumble out, leaving brown hair dye stains all over the upholstery.

After the planetarium I have to stop at the airline ticket agent to make the ticket changes necessitated by our extra day of shooting. When the airline rep discovers I am from Texas she beams at me:

'We *love* Texans! Texans are so *nice*! Not like New Yorkers! Here . . . I've given you the best seat on the airplane with lots of leg room. Can I do anything else for you today?'

I am charmed.

Not so charming are the clothes of New York women. Every woman in New York wears black in the winter. Black dress, black leggings, black overcoat, black hats, gloves and shoes. Mimi explains this to me. New York is dirty and black doesn't show the dirt. Also, black makes you look thinner. As if they could look any thinner.

These New York white women, already a sickly pale from sunlight deprivation, have starved themselves into an austere and *unhealthy* state. There is a paucity of flesh, a meagerness of limb. Their puny little legs on top of those absurd 1970s retro platform-heeled monstrosities they call footwear make them look like starving crows as they stalk around like mourners at a mass funeral. I have become used to the substantial women of the South, nicely padded with a diet of beer and chicken-fried steaks. They should declare this city a fashion disaster area as far as I'm concerned.

Come the sober dawn and it's back to Jersey for another shot at selling diesel fuel additive. This time all goes well and the replacement cans look pretty good. My part consists of coming into the diner in my winter trucker garb and sitting at the counter next to the old trucker and saying, 'My gosh-durned rig gelled up on the pass! Cost me a half day and a thousand dollars to git her towed back!'

This prompts the old trucker to pick up a handy can of Top Dog and tell me what a hopeless nitwit I am for neglecting the latest innovation in automotive science.

All the while the real truckers who patronize our still operational diner set peruse us skeptically.

The climax of our little epic involves me driving off in my freshly ice-protected rig with my faithful dog (Top Dog . . . get it?) at my side.

For this pivotal roll Jay has hired a national champion boxer named Thomas. Thomas is completely inbred, and his life expectancy is about five years. His nervous system is so genetically unidimensional that he quivers pretty much all the time. Maybe he's just scared of the big diesels rolling in to the parking lot. Or maybe his agitation is caused by his owner, a woman who tells me that Thomas's puppies with the correct coloration sell for $50,000. For that kind of coin I suspect his mistress collects Thomas's seed for storage. I guess you'd quiver too. She probably feeds him special oyster Alpo. Come to think of it, maybe that's why he's only going to live five years. I wonder if I'd last that long? As Thomas and I stand in the cold waiting for the final lighting tweak I sink into a reverie . . .

What if Arnold Schwarzenegger started selling his sperm on the Internet? I bet he could get $50,000 per serving, easy. Hell, Arnold could probably get $150,000! Think of how many prospective parents would pay through the nose to endow their progeny with Arnold's terminator genes. He could start a whole new empire! Forget Planet Hollywood. Just stay at home and take a lot of zinc and stock the refrigerator with vials of potential Arnolds and Arnold-ettes.

And what about those super models who advertise their eggs? Some rich couple could buy a couple of those and then apply a liberal dose of Arnold milk and raise these perfect genetic beings! Forget dog breeds! 'And this is our son. He's a Schwarzenegger/Turlington cross!' Instead of saying 'I'm Irish', kids would be saying, 'I'm Schwarzeneggerish!' . . .

'Move it! Move it! ACTION! ACTION!'

Jay is yelling again. I guess I tuned it out from force of habit.

'What's the matter with you! Why are you standing

there quivering? We're ready to go here! I want you to walk Thomas past the camera and over to the truck! ACTION!'

Thomas strains at the end of the leash and drags me behind. He is not really acting but rather responding to his mistress who is standing just off camera and waving something at him.

God, I hope that's a dog biscuit and not a test tube.

Jay picks us up the next morning for the drive to the airport. Jay has previously regaled us with the story of how he once made it from Midtown Manhattan to La Guardia in twenty minutes flat. But today it's snowing and the bridges are gridlocked with confused winter drivers. Jay's driving goes from apoplectic to bellicose to kamikaze-jihadic and on up the scale from there. By the time we get to Queens he has sunk into a stinking funk. (It rhymes!) He searches for shortcuts he remembers from twenty-five years ago. Strangely enough the shortcuts have somehow changed into cul-de-sacs. Nevertheless we arrive at the airport with just enough time to load our baggage on to the curbside and haul ass to the gate.

From my superb airline seat I take one last look at the metropolis below. Goodbye New York, you gritty, sprawling beauty! I've mastered you this time! And I'll be back to take my pleasure again, now that I know all your twists and turns, your peculiar little ticks and mannerisms. Sing it, Liza! Kong comes!

My breast swells with passion until Jay leans over to me . . .

'That's Jersey City. If you want to see Manhattan you gotta look out the other side of the plane.'

Night on Olympus

BACK IN THE OLD DAYS before I became semi-famous I sometimes had to perform certain other types of employment of the not-so-glamorous variety merely to endure so to speak. Being dedicated to the proposition that I was forever and always an entertainer I sought jobs that could still loosely be described as acting. Such as playing Santa Claus. A few times Santa's elf. The dreaded pink stuffed Easter Bunny. No matter the indignity, the money was good and I was developing my craft. Really. One of the agencies I got bookings from was Three Ring Service.

Well, they call me up this year to see if I'm interested in a little Xmas party caper. I feign indifference from my lofty status as an established semistar until they mention the tab for this little gambit. To shorten the torment I sign up to perform at the Dell Corporation holiday extravaganza. I also enlist my wife, Diane, and one of my acting students. Christmas cash.

You may know that Dell is owned by Michael Dell, boy billionaire, who sells computers over the internet and whose stock went up 252 per cent a couple of years ago. Naturally he has to throw a bash to thank the many drones who contribute to his empire. Since he's Jewish he's not really too big on Christmas, so the theme of this year's 'holiday party' is 'A Night on Olympus' starring Michael himself as Zeus. I and others like me are hired to provide additional Greeky type atmosphere. I decide to go as the Philosopher King. Diane has to be Hera, Queen of the Gods. My acting student Collette, five feet ten inches of pale pulchritude and cascading red hair, will portray Aphrodite, Goddess of Love.

Luckily one of the theater companies in town just did a production of *Trojan Women*, so I glom on to a purple cassock and rent the Helen of Troy costume for Diane. This little number is shall we say . . . minimal in its ability to refract light. Gossamery. Peek-a-boo. Transparent in some areas and in others positively absent. I think it's a wonderful costume, but Diane has some reservations. I assure her that she looks deliciously goddess like. She adds some gold leaf clusters to our hair and we think we look very Greekish. I also carry my trusty redwood staff, which I have had since I was a woods hippie in the Santa Cruz mountains south of San Francisco.

It's the night of the party, and we pick up Collette and drive to the Austin convention center. One thing we learn right away is that the Greeks must have frozen their asses. It's the coldest night of the year and the women are barking in outrage at being forced to go naked into the winter bleak. I drop them off and go park. I walk alone down the alleys off Sixth Street in my sandals.

It is almost as cold in the Austin Convention Center, an edifice vast in its inept design. The Dell folk have put together an immense layout as big as the proverbial football field (the basic American unit of measurement denoting anything sizable). The roof is about fifty feet up, leaving quite a volume of air to be heated. It isn't. The decorations are great. They've got huge papier-mâché statues as centerpieces of the opulent food tables. Zeus is throwing big thunderbolts. The capper is a working volcano, four stories high with red flames shooting out and sound effects. For some reason they've hung a lot of fish over the dance floor. We decide it must have something to do with Poseidon.

We meet up with our fellow Greeks. There's the Oracle of Delphi. She's concentrating on the breast aspect of fortune-telling. For effect she is carrying a lit candle in front of her wherever she goes to add a touch of mystery. The security guards soon put the kibosh on the open flame, so she blows it out and continues to carry her unlit and decidedly meaningless candle in front of her as she and her breasts parade around the auditorium.

One of our party has been designated as the mermaid. She has the fish tail over her nether appendages and flops on this long wheeled table as Hercules pushes her around the room.

We have a troupe of toga-ed acrobats. They are having trouble warming up their muscles in the chill.

We have a little guy about five foot three who is dressed in a flesh-colored body stocking with a heart over his genitals and flowers in his hair. He carries a little bow and insists that he has been hired to play Cupid. I say no, this is the Greek pantheon and he is Eros, the son of Aphrodite. Well, he doesn't want to be Eros; he wants to be Cupid. But he likes the idea of being Aphrodite's son and follows the lanky Collette around for the rest of the night. He calls her Mom.

The partygoers are arriving and checking their coats. Our little group of Olympians mingles with the full-length sables and tailored tuxes. The computer business has been berry, berry good.

The basic act goes like this: I walk up to a bunch of nouveau riche techno geeks and say, '*Make way for the Gods!*'

They say something like, 'Lookee there. It's Moses.' (My staff has confused them.)

I say, 'No! No! I'm Greek! I'm Greek! The Philosopher King . . . servant of the Gods! Agamemnon . . . Solon . . . you know?'

The techno geeks stare vacantly. 'Hey! You're wearing Tevas . . . I didn't know Greeks had Velcro! Hardee hardee har har!'

All right, so I didn't go out and buy a pair of genuine Hellenic sandals. I got a cassock, didn't I? Anyway, '*Make way for the Gods! Here is Aphrodite . . . Goddess of Love!*'

Collette steps forward and in her best Greco-Tex accent asks, 'How y'all doin'? Twang 'em, Cupid!'

Eros points his bow at them and goes, 'Twang!' And that's pretty much our act.

Diane has decided that she is underdressed for this affair and spends a lot of her time hiding in the shadows of the Greek pillars and skulking in and out of the volcano. She has a bag of gold glitter, and when I force her to she sprinkles 'the Blessings of the Gods' on various couples. Most of the bespangled women of Dell think that Diane is a fellow employee whose party dress has gone horribly, horribly wrong, and they give her a wide berth. That leaves us walking aimlessly around the vast auditorium in endless circles until midnight.

For some reason, the powers that be have decided that the party will be more fun if nobody can see anything, so they have almost no lights on. Everybody sits at these big round tables and tries to see what they're eating. The women have spent big money on their spangly dresses and want to show them off, so they wander over to the food tables where the only lights are. I suggest to one that she turn in slow circles so she will look like a mirror ball.

The band is some electro-techno-bop outfit that plays dance hits from the 1980s. Everything has the synthesizer throb going full blast and that idiotic drum pound pulse. Drives everybody nuts in about ten minutes. But hey, it's dark and it's cold and the music sucks and they've had a lot of free Champagne and by golly let's party, so all the geeks and their spouses crowd on to the dance floor under the flying fish and throb on.

This leaves us gods and goddesses to hang out and watch the acrobats pull their groins trying to do tumbling runs on concrete.

After a bit the lights come up a little and we see that Michael Dell has taken the stage. He is joined by his wife and children. (They have a set of twins whom they named Zero and One.)

Mike has some music in his hand. Now two of his honchos come up. My God! They're going to sing! This ought to be good. Everyone crowds toward the stage as Michael and the Dells launch into their hit . . .

> 'Jingle Bells, buy some Dells,
> Better take home two!
> 'Cause if you buy a lot of Dells
> That stock will split for you!'

Michael Dell is the King Bee and the hive buzzes with appreciation. He gives a little speech about how good we did this year and how we couldn't have done it without you, the drones and geeks of the world! Keep on pumping productivity out of every pore! This year we're number two, having displaced IBM! But we sell six million a day on the Internet! Next year we take over the world!!

By this time the swarm is in a froth.

Michael lets his kids say, 'Hi,' in the microphone and he says 'Merry Christmas' and 'Happy Hanukkah.' Then he gets down on the dance floor, and he and his wife start doing the dirty bop to the techno-throb.

His swarm joins them in a pulsating communal group-grope, exchanging pheromones in a fierce paroxysm of corporate self-pollination. It's stunning in its force.

We hired entertainers just stand back at a safe distance and watch this National Geographic moment. Egads, no wonder these geeks own the world! They believe!

One of the Dells grabs the Delphic oracle by a breast and yanks her and her candle on to the dance floor. We never see her again.

Diane is hiding in the volcano, trying to get warm and invisible. Suddenly a drunken, bespangled geek-spouse lunges out of the hive and grabs me by the cassock.

'Come on, Moses, let's dance!'

In terror I am dragged into the maelstrom where Michael Dell is feeding his children on the love-sweat of his fattened technocrats. He is doing the Stroll and his employees make grinding motions at him as he courses down their gauntlet of adoration. Somehow I am being led toward his blond wife. I am to be some sort of biblical sacrifice. The Moses presumption has gotten all twisted and they think I am parting the waters for them or something.

Michael beckons me on and now I am techno-throbbing with his wife. It's damn hard to dance in a cassock. I start gesticulating with my staff to cover for my clumsy moves. I break into a Chuck Berry duck walk with my staff as a prop and the whole swarm starts yelling at me, 'Go Moses! Go Moses!'

No escape.

A bespangled Geek-wife caresses my staff and coos at me, 'Go Moses, go!'

I yell back 'Fear Not! My Rod and my Staff shall comfort Thee!'

I hold it horizontally about two feet from the floor and the woman starts doing the limbo in her thousand-dollar dress. The rest of the swarm joins in and that's how I leave them: each end of my staff squeezed tight between the thighs of a large Bee-woman as the Dell-drones limbo ritualistically beneath it in parade before their King Bee Love God.

Diane and I run for it.

I never thought I'd miss the pink stuffed Easter Bunny.

Method Surgery

IN MY ONGOING QUEST for employment I have tried many techniques to make an impression at an audition. I have yelled and I have whimpered.

I have worn long hair, beards, tattoos and fake nose rings.

I have worn prophylactic devices behind my ears to make them stick out.

I have snatched a coffee cup out of the casting director's hand and thrown it across the room.

I have borrowed the casting director's kimono and modeled it for the director. (I looked way cute.)

I have even had surgery.

Surgery? No, I didn't have my eyes done and I don't need implants. Let me explain . . .

I go to an orthopedist and his name is Dr. 'Frosty' Moore. Frosty is an old college ballplayer and I guess he got his nickname because he was a relief pitcher and he'd come into the game and 'freeze' the bats.

I tell him to take a look at my knee, which has been popping out of joint for twenty-odd years. Ever since my college chum got me to test-drive his Triumph 650 one day at Stanford. At the time I had driven a little Honda putt-putt, but that was about it for me and motorcycles.

My friend shows me how to goose the throttle and tells

me to let it rip, which I do, and it does. That monster stands up so fast I do a wheelie into the side of a building before I get my hand off the throttle. I lay there in a crumpled heap as my friend races past me to see if his motorcycle is all right.

Since then I have had a trick knee.

Frosty picks up my leg and twists it one way . . .

'Does that hurt?'

'*Yes!*'

'How 'bout that?'

'*Orrrrg!*'

'And this?'

'*Grawlllfff!*'

'I thought so.'

And he starts laughing at me. Tears come into his eyes as I stare up at him from the cold steel table, baffled. Finally, Frosty says with his best bedside manner, 'Man, you are all fucked-up!'

This candid remark wins him my instant approval, and we proceed to the description of what must be chopped, cut, harvested, trimmed and rebuilt. All delivered with a jolly smile from Frosty, who is either delighted with my naïve bewilderment at the state of my appendage or else with the prospect of a huge fee about to be collected from my insurance company. (One of the happier perks of my profession is a dynamite health plan that pays one hundred per cent of almost everything. All you have to do is make $7,500 under a Screen Actors Guild contract in a calendar year.)

Many MRIs later I give a cheerio to my loving wife as I am wheeled into the ice-cold operating room of St. David's Hospital for the chop job.

I, in the purity of my commitment to natural ways, have eschewed general anesthetics. I will go to great lengths to preserve the pristine and sacred temple of my body from their vile effects. I abhor drugs. Absolutely abhor them. Drugs are bad for you. I know that now. Don't talk about 1968. That was different.

I have carefully prepped my anesthesiologist, and she is giving me a spine block. That's a drug that puts your legs to sleep but leaves the rest of you conscious. Of course it hurts so much to get the spine block that you have to take another drug to render you calm enough for spine blocking. An unfortunate but necessary compromise to the purity of the pristine and sacred temple.

Plunger goes in; you count to ten . . .

When I wake up a few minutes later I have a tube into my femoral artery and my legs are dead.

Frosty has turned on the video monitor so I can watch the show.

I have asked Frosty to speak only positive things while operating so I can program my subconscious mind for health and recovery.

Frosty gets right into the spirit of the thing by picking up what looks like a chainsaw and revving it up out of my sight and saying 'OOOOPS!' Then he makes all these incisions in my leg and sticks his little tubes in there with all the lights and cameras, and we get the video of the inside of my knee.

'Yeecchhh! Oh wow! Would you look at *that!*'

'Waddaya see? Waddaya see?' I ask apprehensively.

Frosty gives me the tour:

'This is what's left of your ACL. Your meniscus is torn

front and back . . . can't even sew that up. This here is the surface of your knee joint and all that stuff is scarring and pitting . . . gonna have to grind that down. You got some kind of bone spur jutting out that's carving on your medial collateral . . . that probably hurts. We'll saw that off. And all this garbage is general debris . . . looks as if this is going to take a while. Might as well get started.'

Now it's Tool Time in my knee as Frosty inserts one diabolical instrument after another into the blasted lands. One has little alligator jaws on it that he chomps away all the cartilage with. Then there's a little band saw number that goes 'Whhiiirrrr-bzzt!' Every once in a while Frosty sticks an electric egg beater in there and froths everything up into cotton candy and then vacuums up all the stuff he's carved out.

Quite fascinating to watch on TV.

Three hours later I am in my hospital room, still feeling no pain. In fact I am starving and they feed me a big meal. I reassure Diane that the whole thing is a breeze.

Frosty doesn't agree. He comes to see me and warns me that due to the large amount of work he's done, I may 'experience significant discomfort'.

I'm still blissfully numb in spine block city.

'No prob, doc, thanks a lot! You're an artist, baby! An artist, I tell you!'

They've put something that looks like an alien exoskeleton on my leg to prevent movement and damage. I lie there stupidly watching TV as the spine block slowly wears off.

Two hours later the anesthesiologist comes to see me and I tell her that maybe I could take just a *little* something for the pain. Nothing that would seriously profane the pristine and sacred temple, naturally. Just a *little* something.

She adds some placebo to my I-V and leaves.

An hour later I am frantically pushing the hot button to the nurse station.

'Alert! Alert! Quick! Bring *morphine!*'

Several shots later, my consciousness is still oozing inexorably south into the panting throb of wounded tissues and freshly sculpted bone.

Although significantly addled, I demand more drugs. They call Frosty at home and he gives the go ahead . . . to bring in the morphine pump.

Wondrous are the ways. This contraption delivers a healthy dose of opiates into my IV every twenty minutes. I have to push this little button on the end of a cord when the computer screen says 'good to go'.

Suddenly I have lost all interest in the TV shows. My gaze is riveted to the morphine pump computer screen, waiting for the magic words that will have me thumb-pumping that button like a lab monkey in a psych class experiment.

This is my life for the next three days.

The nurses are a sullen group as a whole. And slothful. Unforgivably slow replacing my morphine bottle when it's empty. This is what HMOs have wrought. One nurse for twenty beds. I've been here two days and I haven't had a bath or a change of sheets. I've developed some kind of hideous Marat-like skin rash.

Finally I ask Tex, the tattooed night orderly, to sponge my back. It's four o'clock in the morning and Tex and I have been placing bets on my blood pressure numbers. Kind of an over/under system.

Tex likes me. As long as I keep losing money to him, he'll give me all the morphine I want.

I'm seeing funny things when I close my eyes. Cannibal rats chew my leg. Drooling guppy brides entangle themselves in my IV drip.

I feel like a doodlebug sliding down a slippery sand slope into the waiting jaws of the ant lion hungering for the juices of my thorax.

Besides that, I can't pee.

Bloody Mary runs down my options.

Mary is my latest nurse. She's a middle-aged African American woman with a limp. She doesn't like it that I haven't been eating and haven't been walking. (I'm supposed to get out of bed and gimp around on my crutches a couple of times a day to make sure my knee hurts as much as it possibly can.) And now this perplexing irrigational misfunction.

'Well, of course you can't pee, you've been stoned as a goat for three days and everything is shutting down.'

Mary is fairly blunt.

'Of course I can catheterize you.'

All of a sudden I am climbing out of bed, reaching for my crutches and hobbling to the bathroom. Mary and Diane stumble along behind me rolling my IV stand. I wedge myself into the tiny bathroom, adjust my alien exoskeleton and transfer crutches so I can leave my business hand free. I attempt to perform.

Fifteen uneventful minutes.

It doesn't help that Mary and Diane are shepherding my IV stand outside the door, which is cracked open to allow the tubes to feed in. Plus, as women will, they are talk-talk-talking away. Chatter-chatter-chatter about my eliminational ineptitudes.

Here I am, trying to pee with a couple of gabby women standing almost next to me talking about how I can't do it.

I yell at them to shut up so I can concentrate. The sudden sullen silence is almost worse. I know they're out there, listening.

Ten more minutes.

'OK, goddammit! I can't tinkle! Are you happy?'

I give up and stagger back to bed. Diane and Mary don't say anything to me, but I sense their smugness all the same. Mary asks Diane to leave the room. Then she stares at me through her bifocals and holds up a thin glass tube.

'I'm gonna siphon ya.'

I am like putty in her hands.

Nurse Sluggo is another ball of wax entirely. Tough young blond who resents answering my summons.

'Waddaya want?' says Sluggo.

'Well, er, I was hoping you could replace my morphine bottle a little early because I'm coming up on my twenty-minute mark and I don't think there's enough left in there to give me my total legitimate hit.'

Sluggo takes the bottle down.

'I've gotta check your prescription,' she growls as she leaves.

I sit up in bed expectantly, still clutching my monkey button. I fire off a few clicks for effect, just to keep in practice.

Sluggo's back:

'You can't have a new bottle because you're supposed to check out today. Can't start a new bottle on the day you check out.'

'What do you mean? What kind of mumbo jumbo is that? *I'm in pain here!* Give me give me give me I need I need I need!'

Sluggo frowns in supreme disapproval of patients who plead pain as an excuse for their pitiful behavior.

'I'm authorized to give you a shot. No more morphine pump for you. Playtime's over. I got the needle and I'll say when and how much. Who's your daddy now?'

'Where's Mary?' I demand. 'We have a relationship!'

'Shut up and turn over!'

She slams home the plunger. I'm still irate.

'I want Mary! I want Tex! I want ga . . . ga . . . guh . . . guh GUHHHZZZZ!'

Damn it, she broke my wah-wah pedal. Broke it and left.

Why are my fingers blue? Aren't I supposed to be breathing and stuff? Oh hell . . . she ODed me! Hit the buzzer or die! Mayday! Mayday! Icy fingers down my spine!

Sluggo comes back.

'What now, monkey boy?'

'You ODed me! What was that?'

'Demerol.'

'I *hate* Demerol! Thought it was morphine! Dying here! Heart stopping! Can't breathe! Tunnel of Light!'

Sluggo closes the door to the hall. She hovers over me and speaks in a low voice as she checks my blood pressure.

'Stop yelling. I didn't OD you. You're going to get me in trouble.'

Sluggo is desperately trying to figure how to cover herself if I croak . . . she didn't wait long enough after my drip bag was removed to give me the shot. Shooting dull pains down my left arm.

'Just lie there and relax. And breathe!'

She slaps me around a little. (I told you her name was Sluggo, didn't I?)

'Now, I'm gonna open the door and you're gonna be quiet and I'll bring you some more morphine later, OK? If you can't talk just blink twice . . . Good! See? I *told* you you were fine! I haven't ODed anybody in over a year, goddammit! Here's your monkey button. Feel better? Of course you do. I'll turn off the light and you go to sleep. And stop twitching.'

It's dark now, I tried to call Diane, but I couldn't talk. I only burbled. She's on her way down here to take me home. Or to Betty Ford, I'm not sure which.

I hope they let me keep my monkey button.

I have an audition scheduled for the day after I get out of the hospital.

Most sane people would cancel, but in my garbled mental state, I decide that I *must* keep the appointment. It's for a big movie, and movie jobs have been scarce lately.

Besides, I am supposed to read for the role of a knee surgeon. Such synchronicity is impossible to ignore. Talk about researching a part!

I talk Diane into driving me and my crutches and my knee brace downtown.

The only drawback to my plan is the niggling little problem of having eaten nothing but morphine for three days.

I can't read the lines because my eyes aren't focusing too well. Diane tries to read them to me, but the short-term memory is not up to snuff either.

Also, I seem to be falling down a lot. Even propped up on crutches I tend to list to the east or west. Diane keeps grabbing me before I keel over.

Then there's the drooling.

But that's of no real consequence.

This movie is called *Varsity Blues*. It's about Texas high school football and stars James Van Der Beek from that *Dawson's Creek* TV show. Jon Voight plays the crusty old coach.

Diane and I arrive at the hotel where the audition is taking place, and she carefully spoons me out of the car. Twenty minutes later we make it as far as the lobby.

Bad news. The audition room is in a mezzanine area, accessible only by stairway.

Diane runs off to inform the casting director, who appears forthwith.

It's Barbara Brinkley again. I have a track record as far as Barbara is concerned, and she will shoehorn me into just about any reading.

'Sweetie! You're not looking too good. Are you sure you want to try this?'

'Oh yesh. Dejinitely!'

'Beg pardon?'

'De-finitely.'

'OK. You just stay here and I'll bring him downstairs to you.'

Barbara ascends. A few moments later she leads the director down the stairs. They carve a path through a lobby full of curious actors. The director looks distinctly nonplussed.

There's a little office near the lobby, and they secret themselves in its recesses.

Barbara calls me in. I limp heroically past my fellow

actors into my personal audition space. I hear a great gnashing of teeth. They think it's all a ploy and are wishing they thought of it.

Diane aims me toward the door, and I carefully crutch on in there and prop myself up, script in hand. (For appearances only.)

It's a small room, and the three of us are in very close proximity. The director is standing right at my elbow, which is good because he's keeping me from falling over in that direction.

We're supposed to be in a hospital corridor. I, the knee expert, having just performed surgery on the young quarterback, come out to report to the father, girlfriend and coach. Barbara is reading their parts.

'*Your boy is out of surgery, Mr. Harbor.*' *(wanga wanga wanga)*

Jesus. Did I just say that? Surely not. Must be an echo in here.

Barbara just spoke to me. What? Oh. That was the line. Must be my turn.

'*Lance tore every ligament he could . . .*' *(wanga wanga)*

I seem to be pausing. Why am I pausing? There's more lines. I think. Can't see the script. Ooops! Don't look down. Once I start leaning, it's all over.

'*. . . tore every ligament . . .*'

Damn right I tore every ligament. They must feel my pain . . .

'*Going to need more surgeries . . .*' Lip quivering now.

'*. . . over the next few months . . .*' Tiny tears in the corners of my bloodshot eyes.

'*. . . just to repair them all.*' A stricken look of empathy and compassion.

Barbara reads the father's line:
'*How long?*'
With a solemn, dirge-like tone:
'*Minimum year and a half – if ever.*' (wanga wanga wanga)
Silence. Are we done?
I need to lie down soon.

I hear Barbara telling the director that since this parti-
cular scene isn't scheduled to shoot for a month, I should
have plenty of time to heal. He nods. 'He'll need it.'

I hobble back to the arms of my loving wife. Brave lad.
Home to my bed and my little blue pills.

And so a month later I'm in a hospital hallway set, ready to
do this very same scene. I have lost thirty pounds. (The
little blue pill diet . . . I don't recommend it.) I'm wearing
my green hospital scrubs with that ridiculous little green
skullcap on my head. I walk with a limp as I enter the
scene, clutching my very own MRI photos as a prop.

I stumble up to my mark in front of the worried friends
and family of the injured quarterback. They all look so
healthy. James Van Der Beek and that pretty little girl who
will shortly spread whipped cream all over her essentials
for James to lick off. (That scene will sell a lot of tickets.)

I, on the other hand, look like that alien stick figure that
crawled out of the spaceship in *Close Encounters*.

Jon Voight snuggles right up next to me. He suggests a
two-shot. It's not because he thinks I'm such a good actor
that I deserve equal face time with him.

It's because standing next to me, Jon Voight looks
young.

Geek Fest

HEAVEN HELP ME they're everywhere. Crawling in and out of virtual reality tanks. Hovering over computer graphics displays and standing in line to watch the Industrial Light and Magic demo.

They're geeks and they own the world now.

I'm at SIGGRAPH, the world's biggest computer graphics convention. I'm in New Orleans, but who would know? You see one convention center, you've seen them all. Big fluorescent caverns with air-conditioning ducts.

Air-conditioning ducts with no air in them right now because it's setup day and the worker bees don't rate air-conditioning. They're saving that for the conventioneers. New Orleans in August is el-muggo in extremis and everyone is sweating all over their nice new terminals as they feverishly set up the enormous displays with which they intend to entice the masses into parting with their graphics dollars.

This computer graphics thing has gotten completely out of hand, if you ask me.

It was OK to make that liquid metal man ooze around in *Terminator 2* and dinosaurs are very cool, but these clever little guys have almost figured out how to make artificial actors who do everything us flesh-and-bloods can do without needing a Winnebago. Then won't those producers be happy!

They must be stopped!

Meanwhile they're having a convention for these cybernuts so everybody can check out the new stuff. Oh, excuse me. I mean, 'define the prevailing paradigm', 'push the envelope', 'expand the heterogeneous environment'.

These folks get real carried away when they talk their geek talk.

I'm sure you're asking yourself, 'Marco, what's a complete technical non compos mentis like you doing at a Geek Fest?'

Simple.

They hired me!

Yes, despite all their technology these geeks still need a human who can stand in front of a crowd and play down to the lowest common denominator in a naked, visceral effort to *sell computers!*

IBM has a booth here to show off their big brainiacs. Bob and I are doing forty shows in three days to sing the praises of the RS/6000 and other marvels of the silicon fundament.

Trouble is, IBM is still in the Stone Age, graphically speaking. While all the sexy companies like Alias/Wavefront and Industrial Light and Magic and that ilk are showing two-story demos of dinosaurs and space ships charging around, IBM's display consists of me and Bob and a slide show.

Oh, we have a script of course. The script boils down to something like:

'We're IBM! We have big computers! Won't you buy our big computers? They're so . . . BIG!'

Meanwhile everybody at the convention will be out looking at dinosaurs and cybermuffins. (Cybermuffins are curvaceous young women in short skirts hired by software companies to sit on stools in front of their booths and pass out literature to hordes of panting geeks. This is called 'getting out the message').

Right now our crew is having trouble getting our act on line. The problem is too much electronic interference. Our radio signal mikes are on the fritz because other companies keep co-opting *our* frequency for *their* radio mikes. Also, our TelePrompTers go down every other page, leaving us to cope with all the geek talk by memory alone.

Worried IBM brass watch us stumble through our dress rehearsal. The slide show is not coordinated to our script, and pictures of red sports cars accompany our spiel on molecular engineering. Bob actually works for IBM and wrote the script. He's having a hell of a time remembering all the lines he so generously gave himself.

Most of my lines are things like *'Tell us more, Bob!'* and *'Just how big IS it?'* I deliver them from the audience in true informercial style. (Professional shame being something I sacrificed many lucrative miles back down the show business road.)

My main function is to give away the door prize. This is a jazz CD that fits in with our theme:

'Assembling a great graphics solution is like putting together a great jazz mix!'

Of course we have to listen to this same brain-rotting

jazz tape a hundred and sixteen times and we're still in rehearsal. However, if we didn't give away the CD nobody would sit through our stinking little show on a bet. So there you have it.

The other companies are having about the same luck as we are in preparing for tomorrow's opening. The Alias/Wavefront display next door currently features a two-story video with the words 'System Error' starkly centered on the fifty-thousand-dollar screen.

Serves them right for stealing our radio frequency.

I go backstage to see if we can fix the sound. Our techies are wedged into a crevice full of malfunctioning equipment. They're trying to retool the slide show. Forget the sound. I go back to the hotel.

The Marriott is packed with the flower of geekdom. Now that it is evening they are massing for an attack on the fleshpots of the Crescent City. Some of these are readily available out the side door of the hotel where, as you exit, a hawker across the street opens the door of a dive to give you a view of the pole-humpers inside.

As I walk down to the French Quarter, women sidle out and rub their breasts, promising who knows what delights if I only start forking over my Yankee dollars. (These delights will remain undiscovered by your humble correspondent.) The geeks are aquiver, however, as they crowd into the hellholes of the Quarter.

It's going to be some weekend.

New Orleans is quite happy to have 40,000 raving cybers visiting their city in August. It's not exactly tourist season down here on the bayou.

The effect is like one of those nature films where huge masses of migrating wildebeest blunder mindlessly onward while ravenous lions, hyenas and crocodiles cut weaklings out of the herd.

The big event tonight is a free dinner being held at Mardi Gras World; a huge warehouse where they store the parade floats.

I ask for directions in the lobby, and a party of geeks invites me to split a cab. The only hitch is that Mardi Gras World is across the river in some treacherous slum known as Sudan or Nubia or some such name that makes white people real nervous. I don't remember exactly; I was too nervous.

Our Pakistani cabby has no idea how to get there. He knows where the airport is. Is it near the airport? No? Well then, he's helpless. After a long conversation in Pakistani with his home base we take off.

Sure enough, the moment we get across the Mississippi we are disastrously lost. The cabby begins wandering aimlessly up and down streets looking at signs.

Soon we are in a bad, bad place.

We feel somewhat secure only because nobody seems to live here in Sudan. They've all been murdered. We finally see a bum weaving his way down the middle of a side street. We stop and ask him for directions. This makes his day. Somebody needs him! We watch him make the supreme effort to clear his brain enough to help us. 'First you go left . . . Then left at the light . . . Then straight on till morning!'

I really should have tipped that guy.

At last we arrive. My ride-sharing geeks immediately disgorge and leave me to pay the tab. I hope they catch a flesh-eating computer virus.

Mardi Gras World is a lot of fun, except it looks a lot like a convention center with all the geeks running around. Great floats. Big fiber glass heads of Elvis and Marilyn. We eat jambalaya and listen to the swamp band sing about Loup Garou, the werewolf of the bayou. Being alone, I sit down at the end of one of the long tables set up for the conventioneers.

'Hi there! We're from IBM!'

Oh great.

'Hey! Aren't you that guy? Hey look, Iris, it's that guy from the show today! What's with that slide show? Can't you do something about that? It really sucks!'

So went the rest of my evening.

Opening day. The flower of Geekdom arrives. 40,000 strong they come and they all want free T-shirts.

The first six shows are a nightmare of bad mikes and crashed TelePrompTers. Bob finally gives up trying to stay on the script and we wing it. This goes rather well.

Of course the IBM brass watching from the back row may not think so. The main problem is that every time we get the audience actually interested in something about processing nodes or bandwidth stretching, the two-story dinosaurs across the aisle start roaring and everybody laughs.

This goes on for fifteen shows back to back all day. We are whipped puppies. I'd planned to tour the floor and check out the exhibits but opt instead for an early dinner and bed.

Day two goes better. We completely ignore the fickle TelePrompTer and cruise. People are storming our booth trying to win a jazz CD and an IBM T-shirt. We also have an espresso machine and a bunch of notebook computers where people can surf the net. IBM calls this the Cyber Cafe.

The geeks love it, always preferring a conversation in cyberspace above all other forms of personal interaction, save one.

The IBM brass is much happier.

At the end of our shift I check out the competition.

One popular exhibit features a cybermuffin with wires running out of her skintight rubber body suit into a computer bank. As she wiggles around, a cartoon frog on the monitor re-creates her movements. I guess this is supposed to be more thrillingly realistic than just letting some cartoonist draw an animated frog.

The big outfits like Disney seem to be using their presence here as a cover for their recruiting. They cast out their nets and seine the river of geeks and take the fat ones back to Hollywood.

The only connection with New Orleans is a dark hallway called the Virtual Bayou, where several exhibitors have set up monitors inside pirogues with stuffed gators and fake moss around them. They're all selling the same tacky ersatz space age computer crap.

The noise level in the convention hall is appalling. 40,000 people yelling in each other's ears to be heard over the cacophony of bells, whirs, whistles and explosions coming out of all the demos. And the electromagnetic fields in here must be giving everybody tumors. Think of all the electrons bombarding you from machines like our meal ticket, the IBM RS/6000.

As I cruise the exhibits, the hairs on my arm ripple in sympathetic sine waves.

Tonight should be a treat. Bob and his entourage and I are going to Tujagues for dinner.

Tujagues is a restaurant on Decatur Street that's been open since 1850. My folks used to eat there in the 1940s. The waiters have all worked there forever and my parents got to be friendly with one of them named Blackie.

Blackie wound up dropping dead right in the restaurant one night, but not before carefully placing his tray on the floor so he wouldn't spill the étouffée. When I mention this to the current owner, all of a sudden we get the star treatment.

'You knew Blackie?! Hey! Maurice! These people knew Blackie! Right this way!'

We get a private room upstairs and are served in courses with extras thrown in at no charge.

All the bisque we can eat. Triple entrées. Double desserts.

Four hours later we stagger downstairs and out into the night.

We have tickets for the Disney party, supposedly a hot item.

We decide to walk off the crawfish, and our trail leads us into the netherworld of the city. Tarot card readers on every corner. African American children tap dancing for tips. Blind accordionists sitting in alleys where the acoustics are good.

Sex shows everywhere. Actual *stores* for witches. Voodoo shops. ('Honey . . . I'm goin' down to the corner to pick up some gris-gris. Go ahead and tie the chicken around your neck, will ya?')

New Orleans must be the only town in this country that actually features black magic as an *industry*.

I mean, it's in the tourist literature!

'Take the Anne Rice Garden District vampire tour!'

The Disney party caters to the same. It's being held in a convent, of all places, and the theme is Saints and Sinners. Indeed.

The guests are teeming all over this place gawking at the religious artifacts and statues of St. Theresa while that same Loup Garou band from the other night plays the werewolf song and everyone stuffs their face with more crawfish.

Even I am appalled at the tastelessness of these proceedings.

Last day of SIGGRAPH.

Bob and I are now the Abbott and Costello of IBM:

'*The RS/6000 delivers the key applications you need, Bob!*'

'*And it fits seamlessly into your heterogeneous environment, Marco!*'

'*Gosh, Bob! I didn't know you cared!*'

This kind of banter can become irresistible when you've been doing the same show forty times in three days.

The final spectacular is the film graphics award show being presented at a big old theater downtown. As usual it's *the* hot ticket, and all the conventioneers are falling all over themselves trying to get in. The IBM heavies throw a couple of tix at me, so of course I have to go.

The hotel concierge is shocked and appalled that I am actually contemplating *walking* five blocks down Canal Street to get to this theater. Evidently there are people on Canal Street who will hurt me. I am an urban survivor, however, and I assume the protective look of haughty disdain that I learned in New York as I stride boldly down the avenue.

I arrive safely in front of the theater, where the hordes are disgorging from the safety of their tour buses. Everybody has slicked up. In fact the geeks are almost indistinguishable from the movie/music crowd. They all wear black everything.

The fabulosity is excruciating.

The films themselves are a revelation in that I understand almost nothing of what is going on.

The cartoons are 3-D. All the effects are very sharp. It's all so shiny and neat. But everything is so loud and busy and violent and just damn peculiar. It seems that if you are a state of the art computer graphics artist, what you have to do is make as much noise and explosions and real fast jumps as you can so the audience is overstimulated to the point of seasickness.

Didn't anybody ever tell these guys that panning to the left makes the audience nauseated? And they do it every time.

And nobody is allowed to do anything pretty with all this computing power.

If animals dance they must be cockroaches. Heads must explode and disgorge magenta snakes. It's bad trip acid art, is what it is. And the audience of geeks sits there rapt. Worshipful.

One of the films has a narration track that mentions polygon avoidance. Everybody cracks up.

That's when I realize I am totally out of it. Left behind. From the boulevard called relevance I have turned off into a cul-de-sac.

And the geek shall inherit the earth.

The new Paradigm.

The truth doesn't hurt or anything. I'm out of it, but I don't care. Not my MOS, like they say in the Army.

Rave on, you geeks. Take the world that seems to be yours for the taking. I'll be reading a novel or something.

I'll call you up when my computer breaks down and I can't play solitaire any more.

Homage to Smurf Queens

A **LOT OF MOVIE STARS** are short. I think it's because you have to have a lot of fight to make it big and short people learn how to fight from the get go.

Especially men. Tall guys have got it made. Natural selection has already favored them. They're usually good at sports. Other guys don't beat them up as often. They don't have to try so hard to impress women. They don't have to learn to do colorful things like acting in order to get noticed.

So in my completely didactic and statistically indefensible way, I am prepared to say that being short culturally prepares the male to develop the character traits that help him become a compelling actor; traits such as vulnerability, courage in the face of adversity and perseverance in the pursuit of goals.

That's why a bunch of short leading men have scrambled to the top. I take my hat off to them. Their talent has transcended their stature.

Yeah, I know. What about Liam Neeson? What about Clint Eastwood?

Sure, there are a few truly lanky individuals on the silver screen. But actually, they *look* a lot bigger than they really are. That's because the camera swells everybody up. You might have heard the expression 'The camera adds ten pounds'? Well, unfortunately for a generation of anorexic starlets, this is true. But the camera also adds inches. Clever camera angles make somebody 5′ 9″ look 6′ 2″.

Another way to make somebody look taller on screen is to stand them next to somebody short.

And that's where the Smurf Queens come in.

Leading men are the undisputed kings of the box office. And since so many leading men are short, they need a lot of *really* short leading ladies to make them look taller. Either that or stand the males on a box, like they did with Alan Ladd when he needed to kiss Sophia Loren. (If it had been me kissing her I would have been happy to jump.)

It's the Hollywood version of natural selection.

It's not that the Smurf Queens don't deserve their success. It's just that in a pool of hundreds of talented, beautiful women, a lot of them get cast because they match up physically with the lead actor. So these short actresses get cast more and develop into bankable stars.

Just don't call them 'cute'.

Challenger is a TV movie based on the space shuttle disaster.

It's less than a year since the accident, and emotions are still raw. The families of the victims are adamantly opposed to what they are calling exploitation. Nevertheless, NASA has given its permission to use its facilities as a location, and the producers have promised a sensitive portrayal.

They're actually telling the truth. The story centers on Crista McAuliffe, the first schoolteacher in outer space.

But they're also telling the story of Martin Thiokol and how the corporate bottom line and pressure to preserve public image subverts safety considerations. (See Ford Pinto and Firestone.)

To play Crista McAuliffe they need an all-American woman. Somebody smart, warm-hearted and totally charming.
Karen Allen is the perfect choice.
It's a wonder to me why Karen is so underused by Hollywood. I think it's because she's such a natural person with so little artifice that she just can't stomach the bullshit.
At first impression, Karen Allen seems an unlikely leading lady. She's certainly pretty, but hardly a bombshell. She's got those freckles. Her natural expression is one of gentle vulnerability as she looks at you with big, sad eyes. She's more of a kid sister type.
But then she smiles.
Karen's got a smile like Vegas on kilowatt appreciation night.
She's got a smile that makes you want to go home and bake her some brownies immediately.
If you were naked in Nome in November her smile would keep you warm.

I am playing one of the schoolteachers training for the mission who *didn't* get picked to be on the crew of *Challenger*. The rest of the unchosen and I spend a lot of time being taken on tours of the NASA site by the head astronaut, played by Barry Bostwick. I have a few lines, but it's mostly Barry talking to Karen.
Now here we go with the stature thing. Barry is the exception that proves the rule. He's about 6' 4". To get a close up two-shot of him and Karen they have to turn the camera at a forty-five degree angle.

They wind up having a lot of conversations seated at a table.

It's kind of hard to emotionally separate from the fact that a lot of us are playing characters who will soon be dead. It gets especially misty doing scenes with Karen. She's enormously appealing in her own right, and she's playing an extremely likable and charismatic folk hero.

Near the end of the shoot, all of the teacher characters are in a room together awaiting the announcement of which one of us will be chosen to fly on the ill-fated space shuttle.

When they read out 'Crista McAullife', we're all supposed to crowd around her offering congratulations. It turns into a hug-fest. Everybody, male and female, has pretty much fallen in love with Karen Allen anyway, and this is our big chance to grab her and smother her with affection. We've also got a dose of the poignants because we know her character just got a death sentence.

When it's my turn I latch on and plant a big kiss on Karen's cheek. Then I hug her and kiss her again and look her in the eyes and give my heartfelt congratulations speech.

Karen holds my hand, gets right up close to my face and says 'Thank you'. She gives me one of those nuclear smiles.

Then they carry me back to my dressing room for resuscitation.

Hollywood is a fickle beast. Especially so in its appetite for leading ladies. Every year a new crop of ingenues is served up and celebrated on the cover of *Cosmo*. They are paired up with one of those short leading men in the latest action thriller and do the obligatory nude scenes and in a couple of years they are history. Shoved down the maw and spit out, bleeding and broken, to crawl off to some network sitcom or other if they're lucky.

Actresses who have escaped the jaws of the ingenue-eater and endured as leading ladies with sanity intact should be appreciated.

I'm not sure how Valerie Bertinelli did it. She's a former sitcom star and I don't think she's really done that many features. But she's starred in a whole hunk of TV movies, and she usually carries them.

Why not films? Who can explain these mysteries? Valerie is a top-notch actress. She can do drama and comedy. She has perhaps the sexiest eyes I have ever seen on a woman. When I hear the expression 'bedroom eyes', I always think of Valerie Bertinelli.

I mean, let's not feel sorry for her or anything. She's been incredibly successful. I just wish I knew why this woman isn't playing leads in films.

We're doing a TV movie called *Pancho Barnes*. It's about a woman who was an early aviation pioneer. She was a daredevil pilot and wound up running the Happy Bottom Riding Club near Edwards Air Force Base out in California, where Chuck Yeager and the boys were breaking the sound barrier and working on their '*Right Stuff*' chops.

In fact, that *Right Stuff* film is probably why they're making this TV movie. When a big film like that captures the public's imagination, the television industry latches on to the idea like a suckerfish on the belly of a manta ray.

This is one of those movies where we follow the heroine's whole life, from her hot-air-balloon-infatuated girlhood, through the early days of aeronautics with her buddy Amelia Earhart, to World War II and the new postwar jet engine paradigm. Valerie has to keep adding gray to her hair and then taking it back out when they shoot scenes from a different era. This aging thing gets hard to juggle on a TV movie, where the shooting schedule is so hectic.

I play a dickhead major on the early 1940s airbase, where we use sacks of flour for bombing practice. My lame-brain trainees keep dropping sacks of flour on Valerie's ranch, so Valerie gets up a head of steam and comes down to the base to read me the riot act about scaring her pigs.

It's a dicey thing for a leading lady to get really angry on a TV movie. The leading lady runs the risk of becoming 'unattractive'. Looking 'unattractive' in even one scene can start the death bell tolling careerwise. On the other hand, it gets so tiresome being wholesome all the time that it must be a relief to just light into somebody.

Well, I'm an inviting target. I play this unctuous, slicked up, by-the-book military type. In addition, Valerie has to enter the scene covered in white flour. This moods her up for a good mad. They've made her look like the head of a New Guinea taro cult.

She stands over my desk and gnaws my head off. It's more like hand grenade eyes in this case.

The director takes her aside and makes a few suggestions. They call in makeup and adjust the look, then reshoot the scene.

This time, Valerie has toned it down a lot. She's kind of adorably mad. And the flour mask has been reduced to a light dusting on her hair with an insouciant little smudge on the end of her nose. I think Valerie liked letting the dogs out, but this is a prudent compromise with the parameters of prime-time family viewing.

We shoot another, later scene after another flour bomb attack. This time, before Valerie can rip me a new one, my colonel comes out and asks her to hire on as a pilot instructor. That's because we just got into the war and she's the best flier around. A female anomaly in a male-dominated profession. Strike a blow for girl-power, etc., etc.

My friend Bill Bolender plays the colonel. Bill goes to auditions barefoot and in an old T-shirt. Even for suit roles. That's because he has a face like Andrew Jackson. Granite-chiseled, I think they call it. With a face like that, you don't need to wear a suit. With a face like Bill's, the fact that he is an excellent actor is merely a pleasant bonus. Most directors cast him the minute he walks in the room. They don't care if he's barefoot. It's the face they want.

Bill gets to make charming with Valerie Bertinelli while I stand there at dickhead attention. She even bats the famous bedroom eyes at him. It's not fair.

We're shooting the scene where Valerie says goodbye to her pilot boyfriend, who is about to fly off to World War II. Sam Robards plays the boyfriend. This is a spectacular scene where vintage aircraft taxi around the airfield set and a hundred uniformed actors and extras clump around while the stars have their romantic moment. The Big Kiss. The first one in the movie for Valerie. Somehow, her character has gone through her whole life story without being kissed, until now.

As luck would have it, Valerie's husband is on the set for the occasion. Valerie is married to the rock guitar god Edward Van Halen.

For once, the crew is excited. Crews are a jaded lot when it comes to movie stars, but guitar gods are a different matter. They gawk openly.

This is as close to sex as we're going to get in this movie, and everybody is wondering how Valerie and Sam will deal with the (assumed) added pressure of an audience that includes a spouse.

Valerie and Edward haven't been spending much time together, with her on the set. Plus, Edward's touring with the biggest rock band in America. There's the groupie factor. Human fret boards offering themselves up nightly for extracurricular power chording.

Valerie just might be sending a message to her hubby.

Accomplice or no, Sam Robards listens to Valerie deliver her 'I'll wait for you' speech and then bends her over almost horizontal while he kisses her so hard he practically dislocates her jaw. When they come up on 'Cut', we all applaud and start yelling, 'take two! take two!' The director happily obliges and the next take is equally passionate. This goes on for a while until Valerie is wheezing for lack of air.

Edward Van Halen is laughing, but I think he decides he might as well stay over tonight and catch the morning flight out.

Sam Robards is our hero for the rest of the movie. He wins the coveted Clark Gable award, an unofficial prize named for that famous manly man who once told another eminently kissable actress, *'You should be kissed, and often, and by somebody who knows how.'*

Speaking of kissing, Helena Bonham-Carter became a star because of one great kissing scene. It was that scene in *A*

Room with a View where she's wandering around in an Italian field and Julian Sands grabs her and plants one on her.

Good career move. She became an instant art-house queen.

Helena is in Dallas playing the title role in *Fatal Deception: Mrs. Lee Harvey Oswald*, which is a typically dumb TV movie name. It's about what happened to Russian immigrant Marina Oswald after her husband was involved in the Kennedy assassination.

Much as *Pancho Barnes* coattailed the success of *The Right Stuff*, this TV movie rides the wave of furor following the release of Oliver Stone's *JFK*.

If you remember, in that one I played a Texas FBI agent with a bad haircut.

This time I'm playing a Texas bar Lothario with a bad haircut.

Movie hair people love period pieces like this. They get to assert their power and scalp every costar in sight. If you complain, it just makes it worse.

My fellow bar Lothario Michael is complaining. We're both sitting in chairs in the hair and makeup trailer waiting for our haircuts. I go first and take my scalping philosophically. A crew cut with white sidewalls.

Michael takes one look at me and starts howling. He has cultivated one of those long-at-the-neck styles where he can tie his hair back in an arty ponytail. He insists that he can just slick his hair back and hide the excess length under his collar.

Fat chance. The trim Nazis have him in their sights. They produce photos of men's hairstyles circa 1964.

When it becomes obvious that his role is in jeopardy, he negotiates a compromise. They'll let him keep a little on the neck but the sides must go. His last words before the sheers dig in are 'Just don't make me look like *him!*' Meaning me, of course.

In this scene, Marina Oswald, who has had everything she owns confiscated by the FBI, is drowning her sorrows at the local pub. She's sitting on a barstool swilling vodka while we bar Lotharios move in for the kill. There's lots of ad-libbing.

Helena Bonham-Carter is a doozy of an actress. She's got the accent down and you'd swear she was a real drunken Russian. She makes it seem effortless.

These English actors always make fun of us Americans and our obsession with the Method. But they seem to be able to act us under the table anyway. Maybe it's all that Shakespearean training. Builds precision or something. Americans look stupid doing Shakespeare. Give us a role where we sweat and cuss and spray beer all over our T-shirts and we're happy.

Anyway, Helena is propped up there with her vodka, ad-libbing in a Russian accent as natural as can be while we Texans are struggling to keep our *Texas* accents together. She's making us look bad.

The director shoots several takes of the Lotharios jockeying for position around Helena and decides the scene needs some more action. Since they're playing jukebox rock 'n' roll in the background, I suggest some dancing. The director says give it a go.

This leaves Michael out, since he has salvaged enough of his neck hair to render him suitable for face-on camera shots only. He has to remain at the bar, while I, with my

three-hundred-and-sixty-degree early 1960s period-com-
pliant burr-head, drag Helena Bonham-Carter on to the
dance floor for some boogie-woogie.

Since Michael made fun of my scalp-job, it is quite
satisfying to cut into his face time with the star. Petty, I
know. But we costars must celebrate our dirty little victories.

Her initial position on the barstool has disguised the fact
that Helena Bonham-Carter is about five feet tall. She's
shorter than her name. I always wondered why she wears
that haystack hairdo. Now I know.

One thing Shakespeare doesn't prepare you for is hell-
bent-for-leather Texas swing dancing. I am now happily
in charge of the scene. I up the ante on my ad-libs.

'Hang on tight, honey. Who's yore daddy now?'

Helena is so little that every time I turn her around fast
she kind of helicopters off the ground. She makes surprised little whooping noises.

Then I move into the dips. They've got her wearing a
tight little red 'Why don't we get drunk and screw?' dress.
The dips are getting quite interesting. Now Helena is
making piercing little shrieking noises.

Emboldened by her loss of composure, I push the
envelope. Since Helena weighs about as much as a basket-
ball, I lift her up toward the ceiling and spin her around.
This elicits giggles and squeals.

Very gratifying.

The director is all excited now and wants to do more
takes. I keep trying to top myself.

They've got a happy-hour buffet incorporated into the
bar set, and I shimmy over to the table and pick up a stalk
of celery. Why celery? Who knows? Artistic inspiration
should be lived, not questioned. I put the fat end of the

celery between my teeth and apply a double-armed spin to my dance partner, ending in a straitjacket clinch from behind her. Then I waggle that celery stalk around so the leafy end tickles her neck. I am rewarded with the whole spectrum of whoops, shrieks, giggles and squeals.

Paydirt! The woman has lost it! A complete breakdown of the finely tuned precision English instrument!

I just can't get over my bad self. What ho, Miss Bonham-Carter! I got your Shakespeare right *here*!

But as I persist in my celery waggling dirty bop, I notice something.

All those whoops and giggles and shrieks are being delivered in a *perfect Russian accent*.

After the scene Helena comes up to me:

'I say, dearie, that bit with the celery was perfectly *ripping*!'

English actors. I tell ya.

Home Fries couldn't be more American. It stars All-American girl Drew Barrymore. The main location is a drive-in hamburger stand in Texas. And I can't possibly explain the plot.

OK, I'll try.

Drew Barrymore is a poor country girl working in a hamburger stand who gets pregnant with the love child of her middle-aged sugar daddy. The sugar daddy has a jealous wife and two grown sons in the National Guard. His sons chase him down with a helicopter and cause him to have a heart attack. That's on the orders of jealous Mama. Somehow, the incriminating helicopter radio transmissions have been picked up on Drew's hamburger stand drive-through microphone. So the less psychotic son, played by Luke Wilson, gets an undercover job at the hamburger stand to spy out who heard what. Naturally, he falls in love with Drew, not knowing that she's pregnant with his own father's love child. Meanwhile jealous Mama is sending out her other, more psychotic son to find and kill the mistress of her now dead husband.

Whew! I would have hated to be the guy who had to pitch *that* concept at the producer's lunch.

I play a redneck asshole with a pickup truck. It's a whole new direction for me.

Actually, it's a key role. I'm supposed to pull up to the drive-through speaker box and demand breakfast. Drew politely informs me over the microphone that the joint isn't open yet. I take this news badly and begin berating poor Drew and abusing the speaker box. Luke Wilson has to come out and offer to stick my head up my own tailpipe, metaphorically speaking.

That's how Drew knows he loves her!

Without me, how would romance flower?

Our location is the quintessential backcountry Texas town of Elgin. (That's with a hard 'G'.) Elgin is so authentic looking that the movie folks don't have to dress it up too much. This must be my eighth film to be shot in Elgin, Texas. The guys at the gas stations recognize me.

The production has, however, elected to build its own hamburger stand. The poor crew has to spend about a month shooting in that hamburger stand. This is not a particularly location-rich script.

But who cares when you've got Drew Barrymore in your movie? America's Sweetheart, version 2000, blond edition. Julia Roberts and Sandra Bullock feel her coming up fast on the outside. Drew is nicely taking up the reins once held by the likes of Sandra Dee. (She'd hate that.)

They bring me inside the hamburger stand to meet her. I don't see her at first. There's this little kid in my way . . . ooops! That's her, isn't it? Nice to meet you. She smiles and greets me warmly and ever so pleasantly shakes my hand.

What an irresistible human being! You meet Drew Barrymore and you're on her side immediately. You want to take care of her and send her to college and stuff. She's a potent combination of Shirley Temple and Marilyn Monroe. You don't know if you want to *buy* her a lollipop or if you want to *be* her lollipop.

Even dressed in a dirty white uniform with a catsup-stained apron over a distended fake-pregnant belly, there is only one word for Drew Barrymore. (Even though I am breaking my own rule.)

She is cute, cute, cute.

We spend a little time with the director going over the logistics of our scene. First he's going to shoot Drew talking to me over the microphone with my pickup in the background. So I still have to go through all my lines so Drew can time her responses. Then we'll come outside and shoot me while Drew delivers her lines off camera so I can time *my* stuff.

It seems a simple thing. But nothing is simple in the movie world. We'll be here until dark.

I hang out while the crew sets up. One of my students, Gina, is a stand in for Drew. That means she gets to be on the set practically every minute and be treated with about the same respect as a lamp standard. (They always get somebody with the same stature and coloring as the star to 'stand in' when they set up the scene and check lights and camera angles and all that business. That's so the movie stars don't get tuckered out.) I warned Gina, but she didn't listen. I always tell my students not to do extra work or be a stand-in, ever. They think it's somehow going to get them ahead. Lead to a big break or something. What it leads to is exhaustion, poverty, psychological abuse and pimples. That last is from lounging around the craft services table eating junk food all day.

Gina ruefully acknowledges that I was right and that she'll never do it again.

We finally start shooting the scene.

I drive up in my truck and start fuming at poor Drew. I hate getting mad at Drew. But it's in my contract.

The director wants more and more anger and rude behavior. That's to put Drew in distress and make Luke look heroic when he comes out to pinch my head.

I think up a good trick. When Drew keeps refusing me service I pull out my pocket comb and rake it across the speaker. I am told this sounds amazing on the sound track.

Sometime late in the day they finally finish shooting Drew. (Can't blame them for wanting to fill up a few extra canisters with her image.) Now it's my turn.

When asked to get angry, I tend to get overexcited. Like I want to incinerate the set. It's a weakness. The director carefully modulates my performance. I only screw my face up a little bit. And my comb-raking is held back to a few decisive strokes.

We go through several takes of me driving up to the speaker and yelling at Drew. And Drew is right there on the microphone with her lines every time. Even though she's not on camera, she gives me her best shot every take. A real pro.

Finally Luke Wilson comes out and offers to rearrange my cranial compartment so that I can closely examine my own digestive tract. Soon afterward, I rapidly drive my pickup far from that place.

It's a wrap for me, although *Home Fries* will go on shooting for another six weeks.

Two months later there's a knock on my door. My trusting wife, Diane, answers it and is presented with a large bouquet of flowers. On the outside envelope are the words 'Marco Perella'. That gets her attention.

'What the hell is this? Who's sending you flowers?'

There's no way to handle these situations. The best defense is always to play dumb. Which is easy for me at this point because I don't have a clue.

Things don't improve when Diane reads the card. It says:

'Thanks for a wonderful time.
   Love, Drew.'

At the bottom is a big, wet-looking lipstick kiss.

This is a nifty little marital aid, indeed.

It takes about a week to convince my wife that Drew Barrymore undoubtedly sent flowers to every member of the cast after the movie wrapped. She was just doing her America's Sweetheart movie star thing.

Diane finally acknowledges the logic of this, and the dubious likelihood of a tryst between Drew Barrymore and myself.

All the same, when *Home Fries* comes out, she watches it very carefully.

Death in the Wankatorium

I **T'S NOVEMBER**, and the year has not been kind. The wretched little TV movies that they used to shoot in Texas have moved to Canada, where the dollar exchange rate and government kickbacks have lowered the bottom line far beneath even the subterranean levels attainable in our fair state. I hear they're shooting thirty movies in Toronto and another thirty in Vancouver. In Texas it's zilchoid. The big Nada. Double-ought. So when the word comes down that a sci-fi flick is starting up in Houston, every actor in the state responds to the audition call.

This epic is to appear on the UPN network in between reruns of the World Wrestling Federation. The basic plot is . . . *aliens are taking over the world!* (It's a whole new concept.) They call it *MK Ultra*, which imparts no meaning at all to anyone. So they change it to *Ultrakill*, which has way too much meaning. They finally say they're going to call it *Billy Sabbath: Alien Killer*. This pretty much nails it, description wise, since our young cop hero is indeed the possessor of that virtuous name.

I am auditioning for one of the Nephilim, an alien race who might not actually be alien at all but just in hibernation after the last meteor extinction. Anyway, we're back and we're pissed. We want to reclaim our planet from the infectious human vermin who have thrived in our absence.

We intend to accomplish this by taking over host bodies of unsuspecting people (we could be your friends and neighbors!) and impregnating as many human women as possible with our evil alien seed. We then harvest the resulting issue. This is a good excuse to get scantily clad, nubile young women into the cast as breeders.

To hurry the process along we have also hybridized some bees infected with a fast-acting killer virus that will decimate the population of Houston overnight and precipitate a mass panic from which we Nephilim will profit.

The director of this little gem is an actor's director. I can tell because during the audition he comes over and whispers in my ear:

'Keep your eyes wide and flare your nostrils and stuff.'

I follow his advice and get the part.

The trouble begins when I read the script. It's an action flick filled with running and jumping and killing and dying. I am only a month out of knee surgery and can barely walk across the room without doing an impression of Igor, the leg-dragging hunchback. Being highly motivated by poverty, I decide to conceal this information as long a possible. Preferably until they have committed a couple of days filming to my part and can no longer affordably replace me with another Nephilim actor.

Unfortunately, the very first day of shooting involves one of my big scenes. I get the drop on Billy Sabbath in a cheesy motel and torture him until his fellow alien killers come to the rescue, at which point I'm supposed to jump off the second-story balcony and run away with super-human speed. Luckily they've hired a stuntman to do the actual jumping, but when I see who it is I prepare for the worst. It's the same guy I worked with on that *Tornado* picture, where they almost killed me twice. This guy has the best career asset in Texas: He looks like me. Since whatever movie I am in I usually wind up getting spilled all over the screen, he gets a lot of work. He's supposed to do the dangerous stuff, but somehow I always get hurt. I surrender to the inevitable.

At least I get to wear the latest in alien chic: a floppy-collared rayon disco shirt with a shiny silver jacket and wraparound shades.

Billy Sabbath is being played by a Young Turk Hollywood actor from one of those TV shows about the young unmarried struggling with sexual mores in the Hollywood young urban professional universe. (You know the kind: Everybody cracks wise in the office and all the women look starved within an inch of their lives.)

My character used to be Billy Sabbath's cop partner, Brad Dempsy, before aliens stole my body.

We talk about the upcoming torture scene. Billy Sabbath tells me he was just in a John Travolta movie where Travolta actually beat his head in for half a day. He loved it and felt so important like a real Method actor so could I please hurt him a lot so he won't have to act?

I reassure him.

Thereupon we embark upon several hours of very satisfying choking, head banging and jaw dislocating. I say satisfying because your regional actor like me secretly lives for these moments when he can inflict a lot of damage on the Hollywood leads.

The alien killer cavalry arrives and I have to run for it. My stunt double does his jump. He crashes through a real plate glass window and leaps over the balcony rail on to a big air bag. The glass cuts his arms up, but it's all in a day's work for a stuntman.

I think I am going to get off easy, but the special effects director tells me I have to match the jump so he can morph my face on to the body of the stunt guy, making it look like the real me jumping. I have to hang from a bar eight feet up and drop into camera on to the sidewalk and then run away with superhuman, special-effects-enhanced speed. My knees start quivering in anticipation.

I ask them if they can lower the bar a little.

'What do you mean, lower it? What kind of weenie-ass regional wimp actor are you, anyway?'

'Well, how about letting me land on the air bag?'

'No, that'll screw up the shot! What's a matter, scared of heights?'

'Well, I just had knee surgery.'

'Goddamn it! Get the producers over here! Call the casting director! We gotta replace this crippled weenie actor!'

'Oh hell, let's just shoot it.'

I proceed to drop to the sidewalk about ten times and run away with superhuman speed. I throw in a few wide-eyed nostril flares for effect and everybody's happy.

The next morning my knee looks like a diseased turnip. Luckily I have a couple of days off and I get to go back to Austin and get cortisone shots and a knee drain. The juice they take out of my joint is mostly blood. A sure sign of trauma, my orthopedist informs me with ill-concealed glee at the prospect of cherry-picking my insurance policy. Of course, I have to do this movie so I can make enough money to qualify for insurance that will pay for the damage I am doing to myself on this movie. It's a wonderfully circular arrangement.

The lead villain Nephilim is being played by a friend of mine. We worked on *Lone Star* together, and we both reminisce pleasantly about working on that quality film. His character's name is Darrius, but because he wears a snake tattooed on his lower belly (the head tucked provocatively into his pants) to indicate his trenchant villainy, we all call him 'Snake Daddy'.

In order to better spread the alien seed, Snake Daddy has started a men's club where middle-aged gents pay to dance with gorgeous girls. On off-hours Snake Daddy impregnates the women with fast-growing alien fetuses that show in two weeks and are ripe for plucking. Snake Daddy takes the girls to the Nephilim clinic and removes the little Nephilim from their wombs, consigning the mother-hosts to the crematorium.

He puts the baby Nephilim into tanks with lots of tubes in them, and the babies grow into big old bald Nephilim bodyguards in a couple of days.

Of course the alien killers, lead by Billy Sabbath, are raiding the fetus farms and torching our stock. This makes us Nephilim very angry. It makes us want to kill and kill again.

So we have a scene upstairs at the club where Snake Daddy is having an orgy with all the dancing girls. They can't resist his alien charms. Or maybe it's the tattoo. Anyway, they've hired all these kids to be extras and lie around in their underwear and on action start humping one another like a brood of quivering arachnids.

Snake Daddy culls the herd for strays.

How this stuff is going to get on television nobody knows.

They just keep saying, 'It's OK. It's cable.'

A beautiful Latina model is Snake Daddy's main partner for today, and she has bought into the whole 'This part will make me a star!' scenario and is happy to remove bras and make other necessary artistic statements as required. She doesn't have any actual lines, but after about fourteen takes (lots of coverage of the orgy), she starts improvising. The line she comes up with for herself in this situation is:

'Spank me! Spank me!'

Thus she is rendered immortal for the rest of the shoot. For the next month members of the crew will come up to our star and say, 'Spank me, Snake Daddy! Spank me!'

As an under-Nephilim I don't participate in the orgy. My character is a bit of a prude and doesn't actually like to touch the humans outside of an occasional torture session. But I still have a sacred duty to bring alien babies into the world as fast as possible, so what I do is go to the sperm bank. This is where I will come to the end of my delicious alien wickedness, because Billy Sabbath has trailed me to the clinic and is to dispatch me as I am making my donation.

Needless to say I have developed a certain curiosity about how exactly this scene is to be shot. I don't think I can get out of this one by claiming knee troubles. I am further alarmed by the appearance of some fancy disco underwear on my wardrobe rack the day of the scene. The old theatre line keeps running through my head: 'There are no small parts, only small actors!'

First I arrive at the Wankatorium and walk in with my sunglasses:

ME:	I have an appointment to donate sperm.
CLERK:	Been here before?
ME:	Several times.
CLERK:	Third door on the right. Thanks for coming.

Then we move to the wank room. I start to get cold feet, thinking of my mother watching me on TV and suddenly seeing . . . I talk to the director.

'Am I gonna, you know . . . I mean do you want me to actually . . .'

'No! No! *NO!* I mean, it *is* cable . . . but no, I think we'll just do it with a back shot of you from the waist up. Then Billy Sabbath will come in and kill you with cyanide bullets and you'll knock over the video player where a copy of *Debby Does Dallas* will be playing and then you'll die on the floor in a puddle of black alien goo.'

I am relieved.

'Thank God,' I say. 'For a minute there I thought I might be in trouble!'

So I sit in front of the video player with my pants down around my ankles, ostensibly mooding up for my deposit. Billy comes in. Now I have to do my death scene.

Billy will sweep in, grim-jawed, and say:

'All right, alien scum! On your feet!'

To which I will reply:

'No problem. Just let me get my pants on.'

Then I will cleverly go for my secret alien ankle holster and come up with gun blazing, to be met by fiery death at the wrong end of Billy Sabbath's cyanide pistol. (Having superhuman strength means it takes a cyanide bullet to kill you.)

I prepare for my death scene. The stunt coordinator is an old pro in the business. He was the first guy ever to set himself on fire and jump out of a window in a movie. His first assistant worked on the scene in *The Godfather* where James Caan got riddled with bullets.

Unfortunately, the old pro assigns his *second* assistant to work on me. A guy in his twenties just breaking into the business. The second tells me very seriously how he's going to wire me up with a squib that will make it look like my chest is exploding, but will hurt me not a whit. I am dubious. I've been squibbed before and it always hurts.

The director wants me to have a spectacular death in order to bring a surge of joy to the audience that has had to endure my loathsome alien villainy. I've impressed everyone with the depth of my characterization, and the commitment to nostril flaring for which I am so justly famed.

The second assistant informs me that I am to get a *double* squib. Oh, the honor of it all. He tapes a cannon ball of rubber on to my T-shirt under the charge so it will not actually blow a hole in my chest.

We march to the set.

I try to prepare myself for the sequence: Reach down for my ankle gun. Swing it around on Billy Sabbath. Get shot in the heart. Fire an errant blank somewhere near Billy's head but not right at him because the blank wad can still hurt him. Knock over the TV. Sag lifelessly to the floor. Lie there patiently until they apply the goo.

Any time you're ready, Cecil.

The fatal miscalculation is that, as I bend down to get my ankle gun, the rubber padding on my T-shirt with its taped charge swings *away* from my chest. Then when I turn quickly to get the drop on Billy Sabbath, it swings out even *further* from my chest. When the guy hits the switch it's like firing a shotgun without holding the stock against your shoulder.

I am kicked flying across the room.

I miss the TV entirely, but no one is unhappy, because it looks like I really got killed. They crowd happily around me.

'Are you hurt? It looked great!'

Oh yes. I am hurt. There is already an angry red contusion over my heart, which has, I think, for the moment, as it were, stopped.

They drag me into the backroom and unharness me from my rubber death mallet. The stunt coordinator has a few resonant words for the second assistant. The first assistant is assigned the task of sweet-talking me into not suing if I die. The producer insists on taking me to the emergency room to protect himself in case I do, in fact, die.

I may have broken a rib, but I think I will survive. I don't want to go sit in an emergency room for hours waiting to see an intern, but the forces of bureaucracy win out. The producer puts me in his Land Cruiser and off we go.

He phones ahead to some doctor flack and asks him to call the emergency room and tell them we're coming in. Don't want to waste a lot of time getting back to the set.

My chest hurts.

We get to the emergency room, and of course there are fifty people there. The producer storms up to the desk and demands that I be seen immediately.

'We called ahead. We're from Hollywood!'

He thinks these magic words will somehow grease our skids into the curtained cubicle, but the Houston emergency room nurse just laughs.

The producer squawks 'This actor has a very serious simulated gunshot wound!'

The emergency room nurse replies 'We've got three *real* gunshot wounds in here and we don't plan on seeing *them* any time soon either, so take a number, bub.'

Defeated, we go back to the car.

The producer bad-mouths location shoots:

'This would never happen in Los Angeles. People understand priorities out there.'

Back on the set I have to complete my death by being gooed. We aliens spit up black blood and smoke and twitch when we are killed by cyanide bullets. I am a master of all three disciplines. Years of study.

I take a huge mouthful of black Karo syrup and burble on cue. They run a tube up my shirt that pumps smoke into my face. I'm lying on my back, so the syrup runs into my eyes as I burble. The first assistant stunt co-ordinator wipes it out with a dirty paper towel after each

take. He assures me he did exactly the same thing for
James Caan.

The director is not satisfied with my burbling technique. He wants great geysers of projectile black blood
lofting up into camera range.

I take an enormous mouthful of goo and make like Old
Faithful. I twitch like an electrocuted squirrel. I smoke like
flank steak on the grill.

Billy Sabbath stands over me and delivers the eulogy:

'Brad Dempsy. Ex-friend. Ex-cop. Ex–human being.
And now just plain Ex. I have a feeling that cyanide is
my only friend.'

'CUT! Print!'
The crew applauds.

I am disgusted with myself because I feel such a glow of
accomplishment. Everyone is patting me on the back,
telling me what a trouper I am and how great the shot
looks. What a memorable death scene!

I am such a movie animal, I am actually *proud* of my
ability to take abuse. Tomorrow I will wake up sore from
head to foot; my knee throbbing and puffing, my ribs
aching, a two-week bruise starting over my heart. I will
develop a terrible eye infection from Karo syrup and dirty
paper towels. I have just portrayed a character who meets
his maker while wanking. And all this somehow makes me
professionally satisfied.

I am fulfilling my destiny. Spank me.

A few months later I run into an old friend. He's working
at one of the big high-tech firms in Austin. Six-figure

income, stock options and 401–Ks. I ask him how life's treating him.

'Oh, pretty good. If you call spending seventy hours a week in a cubicle in front of my computer screen a life! Hey! I saw you in that alien thing where you got dead and spit up all that black goo. What's that stuff taste like, anyway?'

It's sweet. Very, very sweet.

Acknowledgments

To Molly Ivins, who made me do it. She's an unselfish champion of humor and a dispenser of Maximum Encouragement.

To my agent, Dan Green, who laughed, took me on as a client, and told it to me straight.

To my agent, Simon Green, who became my pillar of diplomacy.

To my editor, Colin Dickerman, and all the people at Bloomsbury who have held the reins with a gentle hand.

To my parents, Paul and Lee Perella, who used their wit and literary skill to help me get organized.

To my partner of twenty-one years, Diane Perella, who only laughed when it was really funny.

To all my acting brethren and friends in the industry. We lived through it together.

And to all my Hoodlum Friends. You read all my letters over the years and now you're stuck with this whole damn book. Thanks for everything.

A Note on the Author

Marco Perella's film credits include *JFK*, *Lone Star*, *Varsity Blues*, and *Keys to Tulsa*. He has co-starred in over twenty TV movies, and was a recurring guest star on the series 'Walker: Texas Ranger.' Marco Perella lives in Austin, Texas, and has just released a CD of original songs called 'Carry Me Home'. You can listen to it, read new stories, and correspond with him at www.marcoperella.com.

A Note on the Type

The text of this book is set in Bembo. This type was first used in 1495 by the Venetian printer Aldus Manutius for Cardinal Bembo's *De Aetna*, and was cut for Manutius by Francesco Griffo. It was one of the types used by Claude Garamond (1480–1561) as a model for his Romain de L'Université, and so it was the forerunner of what became standard European type for the following two centuries. Its modern form follows the original types and was designed for Monotype in 1929.